THE

FORLORN DEMON

DIDACTIC AND CRITICAL

ESSAYS

Allen Tate

Essay Index Reprint Series

 BOOKS FOR LIBRARIES PRESS
FREEPORT, NEW YORK

STANDARD BOOK NUMBER:
8369-1483-X

LIBRARY OF CONGRESS CATALOG CARD NUMBER:
70-105041

PRINTED IN THE UNITED STATES OF AMERICA

To
SAMUEL HOLT MONK

On Cares like these if Length of days attend,
May Heav'n, to bless those days, preserve my Friend.

Preface

In one of these essays I call Poe a "forlorn demon in the glass." It is an unhappy phrase that I had thought was entirely mine until the other day, when I remembered the rather bad poem, parts of which I reproduce opposite the title-page. The poem, which is entitled "Alone," has never been famous, and even Poe's authorship has been questioned. But I am sure that it is by Poe, as I am sure that a friend is who he is without the proof of his driver's license or social-security card. If it is not by Poe, no matter; it gave me the phrase and it serves my purpose.

To the question, What would attract the attention of demons if they lost interest in us? we have no answer at present; nor can we guess how different their personalities seem to them; perhaps every demon is sure that he is unique. Poe was certain all his life that he was not like anybody else. The saints tell us that confident expectancy of damnation is a more insidious form of spiritual pride than certainty of salvation. The little we know of hell is perhaps as follows: it promptly *adjusts* and *integrates* its willing victims into a standardized monotony, in which human suffering, its purpose thus denied, begins to sound like the knock of an unoiled piston. A famous literary critic predicted years ago that our poetry would soon echo the rhythms of the internal combustion engine, and he produced a short verse-play to prove it. I take it he meant that poetry would no longer move to the rhythms of the heart, which are iambic or trochaic, depending on whether the ear picks up the beat at the diastole or the systole, with occasional fibrillations and inverted T-waves to delight the ear and to remind us of the hour of our death. The rapidity of a piston reminds us of a machine which can temporarily or permanently break down; but it can be exactly duplicated and it cannot die. To this god, I believe, we owe our worship of *rapid* and exciting language, an idolatry that in one degree or another is the subject of most of these essays.

Sometimes I think that life is a dream, and that what I am really doing is not what I do. I sit, in doubt between waking and sleeping, on the keel of a capsized boat, eating barnacles with my old friend Arthur Gordon Pym and pretending that the hull is a continent.

The reader has been warned on the title-page to expect in these essays a certain didacticism. It is not aimed at the reader; it is home-work, the tone I take when I talk to myself. I published my first essay twenty-five years ago. Since then, year after year, I have been conducting an unfinished education in public. All essayists seem to do this; unlike the scholars, they cannot wait until they have made up their minds before they speak. I am a little perplexed by my failure to understand why I continue to do it. The modern man of letters, if he is not a play-boy, is an eccentric: he is "off centre," away from his fellow citizen who is sure that he is standing in the Middle. I do not know why an eccentric should give himself away by appearing in public; he might do better to stay at home with his family and invite his friends to dinner. Yet once he appears he will appear again and again. Isn't his delighted audience convinced (as he is) that his manners are unique? He thinks he hopes that he is not like anybody else. What he really

PREFACE

hopes is that what made him an eccentric—a committed
sin, a sin desired but resisted, the musty smell of his grandmother's house, one of William Empson's "missing dates,"
an *intermittence du coeur*, or something else quite ordinary
—will not be detected by anybody, even by his intimate
friends. But it always is.

November 14, 1952   A. T.

ACKNOWLEDGEMENTS

(TO THE ORIGINAL EDITION)

The essays in this book were previously published in the following magazines, and are reprinted here with permission:

The Hudson Review: The Man of Letters in the Modern World; To Whom Is the Poet Responsible?; Longinus and the "New Criticism".

The American Review: Modern Poets and Conventions.

The Kenyon Review: The Angelic Imagination; The Symbolic Imagination; Johnson on the Metaphysical Poets; a Note on Critical "Autotelism".

Partisan Review: Our Cousin, Mr. Poe; Is Literary Criticism Possible?; Ezra Pound and the Bollingen Prize.

The New Republic: Crane: The Poet as Hero.

The Sewanee Review: The Point of Dying.

Special thanks are due the Bollingen Foundation, Inc., for permission to reprint "Longinus and the 'New Criticism'" from *Lectures in Criticism* (Pantheon Books), copyright 1949 by the Bollingen Foundation, Inc., "Bollingen Series XVI".

CONTENTS

. . .

From every depth of good and ill
The mystery which binds me still—
From the thunder and the storm
And the cloud that took the form
(When the rest of Heaven was blue)
Of a demon in my view.

—Edgar Allan Poe

1

The Man of Letters in
the Modern World[1]

To the question, What should the man of letters be in our time, we should have to find the answer in what we need him to do. He must do first what he has always done: he must recreate for his age the image of man, and he must propagate standards by which other men may test that image, and distinguish the false from the true. But at our own critical moment, when all languages are being debased by the techniques of mass-control, the man of letters might do well to conceive his responsibility more narrowly. He has an immediate responsibility, to other men no less than to himself, for the vitality of language. He must distinguish the difference between mere communication —of which I shall later have more to say—and the rediscovery of the human condition in the living arts. He must discriminate and defend the difference between mass com-

1. The Phi Beta Kappa Address, University of Minnesota, May 1, 1952. Excerpts from this paper were read at the International Exposition of the Arts, under the auspices of the Congress for Cultural Freedom, Paris, May 21, 1952.

munication, for the control of men, and the knowledge of man which literature offers us for human participation.

The invention of standards by which this difference may be known, and a sufficient minority of persons instructed, is a moral obligation of the literary man. But the actuality of the difference does not originate in the critical intelligence as such; it is exemplified in the specific forms of the literary arts, whose final purpose, the extrinsic end for which they exist, is not the control of other persons, but self-knowledge. By these arts, one means the arts without which men can live, but without which they cannot live well, or live as men. To keep alive the knowledge of ourselves with which the literary arts continue to enlighten the more ignorant portion of mankind (among whom one includes oneself), to separate them from other indispensable modes of knowledge, and to define their limits, is the intellectual and thus the social function of the writer. Here the man of letters is the critic.

The edifying generality of these observations is not meant to screen the difficulties that they will presently encounter in their particular applications. A marked difference between communication and communion I shall be at some pains to try to discern in the remarks that follow. I shall try to explore the assertion: Men in a dehumanized society may communicate, but they cannot live in full communion. To explore this I must first pursue a digression.

What happens in one mind may happen as influence or coincidence, in another; when the same idea spreads to two or more minds of considerable power, it may eventually explode, through chain reaction, in a whole society; it may dominate a period or an entire epoch.

When René Descartes isolated thought from man's total being he isolated him from nature, including his own nature; and he divided man against himself. (The demonology which attributes to a few persons the calamities of mankind is perhaps a necessary convention of economy in discourse.) It was not the first time that man had been at war with himself: there was that first famous occasion of immemorial antiquity: it is man's permanent war of internal nerves. Descartes was only the new strategist of our own phase of the war. Men after the seventeenth century would have been at war with themselves if Descartes had never lived. He chose the new field and forged the new weapons. The battle is now between the dehumanized society of secularism, which imitates Descartes' mechanized nature, and the eternal society of the communion of the human spirit. The war is real enough; but again one is conscious of an almost mythical exaggeration in one's description of the combatants. I shall not condescend to Descartes by trying to be fair to him. For the battle is being fought, it has always been fought by men few of whom have heard of Descartes or any other philosopher.

Consider the politician, who as a man may be as good as his quiet neighbor. If he acts upon the assumption (which he has never heard of) that society is a machine to be run efficiently by immoral—or, to him a-moral—methods, he is only exhibiting a defeat of the spirit that he is scarcely conscious of having suffered. Now consider his fellow-citizen, the knowing person, the trained man of letters, the cunning poet in the tradition of Poe and Mallarmé. If this person (who perhaps resembles ourselves) is aware of more, he is able to do less, than the politician, who does not know what he is doing. The man of letters sees that modern societies are machines, even if he thinks that they ought not to be: he is convinced that in its intractable Manicheeism, society cannot be redeemed. The shadowy political philosophy of modern literature, from Proust to Faulkner, is, in its moral origins, Jansenist: we are disciples of Pascal, the merits of whose Redeemer were privately available but could not affect the operation of the power-state. While the politician, in his cynical innocence, uses society, the man of letters disdainfully, or perhaps even absentmindedly, withdraws from it: a withdrawal that few persons any longer observe, since withdrawal has become the social convention of the literary man, in which society, in so far as it is aware of him, expects him to conduct himself.

It is not improper, I think, at this point, to confess that I have drawn in outline the melancholy portrait of the man who stands before you. Before I condemn him I wish to examine another perspective, an alternative to the double retreat from the moral centre, of the man of action and the man of letters, that we have completed in our time. The alternative has had at least the virtue of recommending the full participation of the man of letters in the action of society.

The phrase, "the action of society," is abstract enough to disarm us into supposing that perhaps here and there in the past, if not uniformly, men of letters were hourly participating in it: the supposition is not too deceptive a paralogism, provided we think of society as the City of Augustine and Dante, where it was possible for men to find in the temporal city the imperfect analogue to the City of God. (The Heavenly City was still visible, to Americans, in the political economy of Thomas Jefferson.) What we, as literary men, have been asked to support, and what we have rejected, is the action of society as *secularism*, or the society that substitutes means for ends. Although the idolatry of the means has been egregious enough in the West, we have not been willing to prefer the more advanced worship that prevails in Europe eastward of Berlin, and in Asia. If we can scarcely imagine a society like the Russian, deliberately committing itself to secularism, it is no doubt because we cannot easily believe that men will prefer barbarism to civilization. They come to prefer the senility (which resembles the adolescence) and the irresponsibility, of the barbarous condition of man, without quite foreseeing what else they will get out of it. Samuel Johnson said of chronic drunkenness: "He who makes a beast of himself gets rid of the pain of being a man." There is perhaps no anodyne for the pains of civilization but savagery. What men may get out of this may be seen in the western world today, in an intolerable psychic crisis expressing itself as a political crisis.

The internal crisis, whether it precede or follow the political, is inevitable in a society that multiplies means without ends. Man is a creature that in the long run has got to believe in order to know, and to know in order to do. For doing without knowing is machine behavior, illiberal and servile routine, the secularism with which man's specific destiny has no connection. I take it that we have sufficient evidence, generation after generation, that man will never be completely or permanently enslaved. He will rebel, as he is rebelling now, in a shocking variety of "existential" disorders, all over the world. If his *human* nature as such cannot participate in the action of society, he will not capitulate to it, if that action is inhuman: he will turn in upon himself, with the common gesture which throughout history has vindicated the rhetoric of liberty: "Give me liberty or give me death." Man may destroy himself but he will not at last tolerate anything less than his full human condition. Pascal said that the "sight of cats or rats is enough to unhinge the reason"—a morbid prediction of our contemporary existential philosophy, a modernized Dark Night of Sense. The impact of mere sensation, even of "cats and rats" (which enjoy the innocence of their perfection in the order of nature)—a simple sense-perception from a world no longer related to human beings will nourish a paranoid philosophy of despair. Blake's "hapless soldier's sigh," Poe's "tell-tale heart," Rimbaud's nature careening in a "drunken boat," Eliot's woman "pulling her long black hair," are qualities of the life of Baudelaire's *fourmillante Cité*, the secularism of the swarm, of which we are the present citizens.

Is the man of letters alone doomed to inhabit that city? No, we are all in it—the butcher, the baker, the candlestick-maker, and the banker and the statesman. The special awareness of the man of letters, the source at once of his Gnostic arrogance and of his Augustinian humility, he brings to bear upon all men alike: his hell has not been "for those other people": he has reported his own. His report upon his own spiritual condition, in the last hundred years, has misled the banker and the statesman into the illusion that they have no hell because, as secularists, they have lacked the language to report it. What you are not able to name therefore does not exist—a barbarous disability, to which I have already alluded. There would be no hell for modern man if our men of letters were not calling attention to it.

But it is the business of the man of letters to call attention to whatever he is able to see: it is his function to create what has not been hitherto known and, as critic, to discern its modes. I repeat that it is his duty to render the image of man as he is in his time, which, without the man of letters, would not otherwise be known. What modern literature has taught us is not merely that the man of letters has not participated fully in the action of society; it has taught us that nobody else has either. It is a fearful lesson. The roll-call of the noble and sinister characters, our ancestors and our brothers, who exemplify the lesson, must end in a shudder: Julien Sorel, Emma Bovary, Captain Ahab, Hepzibah Pyncheon, Roderick Usher, Lambert Strether, Baron de Charlus, Stephen Dedalus, Joe Christmas—all these and more, to say nothing of the precise probing of their, and our, sensibility, which is modern poetry since Baudelaire. Have men of letters perversely invented these horrors? They are rather the inevitable creations of a secularized society, the society of means without ends, in which nobody participates with the full substance of his humanity. It is the society in which everybody acts his part (even when he is most active) in the plotless drama of withdrawal.

I trust that nobody supposes that I see the vast populations of Europe and America scurrying, each man to his tree, penthouse or cave, and refusing to communicate with other men. Humanity was never more gregarious, and never before heard so much of its own voice. Is not then the problem of communication for the man of letters very nearly solved? He may sit in a sound-proof room, in shirtsleeves, and talk at a metal object resembling a hornet's nest, throwing his voice, and perhaps also his face, at 587,-000,000 people, more or less, whom he has never seen, and whom it may not occur to him that in order to love, he must have a medium even less palpable than air.

What I am about to say of communication will take it for granted that men cannot communicate by means of sound over either wire or air. They have got to communicate through love. Communication that is not also communion is incomplete. We *use* communication; we *participate* in communion. "All the certainty of our knowledge," says Coleridge, "depends [on this]; and this becomes intelligible to no man by the ministry of mere words from without. The medium, by which spirits understand each other, is not the surrounding air; but the *freedom* which they possess in common." (The italics are Coleridge's.) Neither the artist nor the statesman will communicate fully again until the rule of love, added to the rule of law, has liberated him. I am not suggesting that we all have an obligation of *personal* love towards one another. I regret that I must be explicit about this matter. No man, under any political dispensation known to us, has been able to avoid hating other men by deciding that it would be a "good thing" to love them; he loves his neighbor, as well as the man he has never seen, only through the love of God. "He that saith that he is in the light, and hateth his brother, is in darkness even until now."

I confess that to the otiose ear of the tradition of Poe and Mallarmé the simple-minded Evangelist may seem to offer something less than a solution to the problem of communication. I lay it down as a fact, that it is the only solution. "We must love one another or die," Mr. Auden wrote more than ten years ago. I cannot believe that Mr. Auden was telling us that a secularized society cannot exist; it obviously exists. He was telling us that a society which has once been religious cannot, without risk of spiritual death, preceded by the usual agonies, secularize itself. A society of means without ends, in the age of technology, so multiplies the means, in the lack of anything better to do, that it may have to scrap the machines as it makes them; until our descendants will have to dig themselves out of one rubbish heap after another and stand upon it, in order to make more rubbish to make more standing-room. The surface of nature will then be literally as well as morally concealed from the eyes of men.

Will congresses of men of letters, who expect from their conversations a little less than mutual admiration, and who achieve at best toleration of one another's personalities, mitigate the difficulties of communication? This may be

doubted, though one feels that it is better to gather together in any other name than that of Satan, than not to
gather at all. Yet one must assume that men of letters will
not love one another personally any better than they have
in the past. If there has been little communion among
them, does the past teach them to expect, under perfect
conditions (whatever these may be), to communicate their
works to any large portion of mankind? We suffer, though
we know better, from an ignorance which lets us entertain
the illusion that in the past great works of literature were
immediately consumed by entire populations. It has never
been so; yet dazzled by this false belief, the modern man
of letters is bemused by an unreal dilemma. Shall he per-
sist in his rejection of the existential "cats and rats" of
Pascal, the political disorder of the West that "unhinges
the reason"; or shall he exploit the new media of mass
"communication"—cheap print, radio and television? For
what purpose shall he exploit them?

The dilemma, like evil, is real to the extent that it
exists as privative of good: it has an impressive "existential" actuality: men of letters on both sides of the Atlantic
consider the possible adjustments of literature to a mass
audience. The first question that we ought to ask ourselves
is: *What* do we propose to communicate to *whom?*

I do not know whether there exists in Europe anything
like the steady demand upon American writers to "communicate" quickly with the audience that Coleridge knew
even in his time as the "multitudinous Public, shaped into
personal unity by the magic of abstraction." The American
is still able to think that he sees in Europe—in France, but
also in England—a closer union, in the remains of a unified
culture, between a sufficiently large public and the man of
letters. That Alexis St.-Leger Leger, formerly Permanent
Secretary of the French Foreign Office, could inhabit the

same body with St.-John Perse, a great living French poet, points to the recent actuality of that closer union; while at the same time, the two names for the two natures of the one person suggest the completion of the Cartesian disaster, the fissure in the human spirit of our age; the inner division creating the outer, and the eventual loss of communion.

Another way of looking at the question, *What* do we propose to communicate to *whom?* would eliminate the dilemma, withdrawal *or* communication. It disappears if we understand that literature has never communicated, that it cannot *communicate*: from this point of view we see the work of literature as a participation in communion. Participation leads naturally to the idea of the common experience. Perhaps it is not too grandiose a conception to suggest that works of literature, from the short lyric to the long epic, are the recurrent discovery of the human communion *as experience,* in a definite place and at a definite time. Our unexamined theory of literature as communication could not have appeared in an age in which communion was still possible for any appreciable majority of persons. The word communication presupposes the victory of the secularized society of means without ends. The poet, on the one hand, shouts to the public, on the other (some distance away), not the rediscovery of the common experience, but a certain pitch of sound to which the well-conditioned adrenals of humanity obligingly respond.

The response is not the specifically human mode of behavior; it is the specifically animal mode, what is left of man after Occam's razor has cut away his humanity. It is a tragedy of contemporary society that so much of democratic social theory reaches us in the language of "drive," "stimulus," and "response." This is not the language of freemen, it is the language of slaves. The language of freemen substitutes for these words, respectively, *end, choice,* and *discrimination.* Here are two sets of analogies, the one sub-rational and servile, the other rational and free. (The analogies in which man conceives his nature at different historical moments is of greater significance than his political rhetoric.) When the poet is exhorted to communicate, he is being asked to speak within the orbit of an analogy that assumes that genuine communion is impossible: does not the metaphor hovering in the rear of the word communication isolate the poet before he can speak? The poet at a microphone desires to sway, affect, or otherwise influence a crowd (not a community) which is then addressed as if it were permanently over *there*—not *here,* where the poet himself would be a member of it; he is not a member, but a mere part. He stimulates his audience—which a few minutes later will be stimulated by a news-commentator, who reports the results of a "poll," as the Roman *pontifex* under Tiberius reported the color of the entrails of birds,— the poet thus elicits a response, in the context of the preconditioned "drives" ready to be released in the audience. Something may be said to have been transmitted, or *communicated;* nothing has been shared, in a new and illuminating intensity of awareness.

One may well ask what these observations have to do with the man of letters in the modern world? They have nearly everything to do with him, since, unless I am wholly mistaken, his concern is with what has not been previously known about our present relation to an unchanging source of knowledge, and with our modes of apprehending it. In the triad of *end, choice,* and *discrimination,* his particular responsibility is for the last; for it is by means of discrimination, through choice, towards an end, that the general intelligence acts. The general intelligence is the intelligence of the man of letters: he must not be committed to the illiberal specializations that the nineteenth century has proliferated into the modern world: specializations in which means are divorced from ends, action from sensibility, matter from mind, society from the individual, religion from moral agency, love from lust, poetry from thought, communion from experience, and mankind in the commmunity from men in the crowd. There is literally no end to this list of dissociations because there is no end, yet in sight, to the fragmenting of the western mind. The modern man of letters may, as a man, be as thoroughly the victim of it as his conditioned neighbor. I hope it is understood that I am not imputing to the man of letters a personal superiority; if he is luckier than his neighbors, his responsibility, and his capacity for the shattering peripeties of experience, are greater: he is placed at the precarious centre of a certain liberal tradition, from which he is as strongly tempted as the next man, to escape. This tradition has only incidental connections with political liberalism and it has none with the power-state; it means quite simply the freedom of the mind to discriminate the false from the true, the experienced knowledge from its verbal imitations. His critical responsibility is thus what it has always been—the recreation and the application of literary standards, which in order to be effectively literary, must be more than literary. His task is to preserve the integrity, the purity, and the reality of language wherever and for whatever purpose it may be used. He must approach his task through the letter—the letter of the poem, the letter of the politician's speech, the letter of the law; for the use of the letter is in the long run our one indispensable test of the actuality of our experience.

The letter then is the point to which the man of letters directs his first power, the power of discrimination. He will ask: Is there in this language genuine knowledge of our human community—or of our lack of it—that we have not had before? If there is, he will know that it is liberal language, the language of freemen, in which a choice has been made towards a probable end for man. If it is not language of this order, if it is the language of mere communication, of mechanical analogies in which the two natures of man are isolated and dehumanized, then he will know that it is the language of men who are, or who are waiting to be, slaves.

If the man of letters does not daily renew his dedication to this task, I do not know who else may be expected to undertake it. It is a task that cannot be performed today in a society that has not remained, in certain senses of the word that we sufficiently understand, democratic. We enjoy the privileges of democracy on the same terms as we enjoy other privileges: on the condition that we give something back. What the man of letters returns in exchange for his freedom is the difficult model of freedom for his brothers, Julien Sorel, Lambert Strether, and Joe Christmas, who are thus enjoined to be likewise free, and to sustain the freedom of the man of letters himself. What he gives back to society often enough carries with it something that a democratic society likes as little as any other: the courage to condemn the abuses of democracy, more particularly to *discriminate* the usurpations of democracy that are perpetrated in the name of democracy.

That he is permitted, even impelled by the democratic condition itself, to publish his discriminations of the staggering abuses of language, and thus of choices and ends, that vitiate the cultures of western nations, is in itself a consideration for the second thought of our friends in

Europe. Might they not in the end ill prefer the upper millstone of Russia to the nether of the United States? Our formidable economic and military power—which like all secular power the man of letters must carry as his Cross; our bad manners in Europe; our ignorance of the plain fact that we can no more dispense with Europe than almighty Rome could have lived without a reduced Greece; our delusion that we are prepared to "educate" Europe in "democracy" by exporting dollars, gadgets, and sociology —to say nothing of the boorish jargon of the State Department;—all this, and this is by no means all, may well tempt (in the words of Reinhold Niebuhr) "our European friends to a virtual Manicheeism and to consign the world of organization to the outer darkness of barbarism." But it should be pointed out, I think, to these same European brothers, that the darkness of this barbarism still shows forth at least one light which even the black slaves of the Old South were permitted to keep burning, but which the white slaves of Russia are not: I mean the inalienable right to talk back: of which I cite the present discourse as an imperfect example.

The man of letters has, then, in our time a small but critical service to render to man: a service that will be in the future more effective than it is now, when the cult of the literary man shall have ceased to be an idolatry. Men of letters and their followers, like the *parvenu* gods and their votaries of decaying Rome, compete in the dissemination of distraction and novelty. But the true province of the man of letters is nothing less (as it is nothing more) than culture itself. The state is the mere operation of society, but culture is the way society lives, the material medium through which men receive the one lost truth which must be perpetually recovered: the truth of what

THE MAN OF LETTERS IN THE MODERN WORLD

Jacques Maritain calls the "supra-temporal destiny" of man. It is the duty of the man of letters to supervise the culture of language, to which the rest of culture is subordinate, and to warn us when our language is ceasing to forward the ends proper to man. The end of social man is communion in time through love, which is beyond time.

2

To Whom Is the Poet Responsible?[1]

AND FOR WHAT? The part of the question that I have used as the title has been widely asked in our generation. I have seldom heard anybody ask the second part: *For what?* I shall have to assume, without elucidating it, a certain moral attitude towards the idea of responsibility which is perhaps as little popular in our time as the accused poetry that has given rise to the controversy. Thus I take it for granted that nobody can be held generally responsible, for if our duties are not specific they do not exist. It was, I think, the failure to say what the modern poet was responsible *for* that made it easy to conclude, from the attacks ten years ago by Mr. MacLeish and Mr. Van Wyck Brooks, that in some grandiose sense the poet should be held responsible to society for everything that nobody else was paying any attention to. The poet was saddled with a total responsibility for the moral, political, and social well-being; it was pretty clearly indicated that had he

1. A brief version of this paper was read at Bennington College on April 16, 1950; present text, at a symposium of the American Committee for Cultural Freedom, May 10, 1951.

behaved differently at some indefinite time in the near or remote past the international political order itself would not have been in jeopardy, and we should not perhaps be at international loggerheads today. We should not have had the Second World War, perhaps not even the first.

The historic political suspicion of poetry is one thing; but the attacks that I have alluded to were by men of letters, one of them a poet—and this is another thing altogether. I do not know to what extent the Marxist atmosphere of the thirties influenced the attacks. In trying to get to the bottom of them one may dismiss too quickly the Communist party-line as a perversion of the original Platonic rejection of poetry which holds that the arts of sensible imitation are a menace to the political order. One must dismiss it respectfully, because it contains a fundamental if one-eyed truth: that is to say, from Plato on there is in this tradition of thought the recognition that however useful poetry may be as a civilizing virtue, it should not be allowed to govern the sensibility of persons who run the state. One may scarcely believe that Sophocles *as poet* was appointed *strategos* in the Samian war, even though that honorific office followed upon the great success of the *Antigone* in the Dionysia of 440 B.C. What I am getting at here is that, were we confronted with an unreal choice, it would be better to suppress poetry than to misuse it, to expect of it an order of action that it cannot provide. (Stalinist Russia seems to do both: it suppresses poetry and supports party verse.) In any literary history that I have read there is no record of a poet receiving and exercising competently high political authority. Milton wrote Cromwell's Latin correspondence, and tracts of his own; but he was never given power; and likewise his successor, Andrew Marvell. We have read some of Shelley's more heroic assertions, in "The Defense of Poetry," into the past, where we substitute what Shelley said ought to have been for what was. The claim that poets are "unacknowledged legislators" is beyond dispute, if we understand that as legislators they should remain unacknowledged and not given the direction of the state. This limit being set, we are ready to understand what Shelley had really to say—which is the true perception that there is always a reciprocal relation between life and art, at that point at which life imitates art.

If poetry makes us more conscious of the complexity and meaning of our experience, it may have an eventual effect upon action, even political action. The recognition of this truth is not an achievement of our own age; it is very old. Our contribution to it I take to be a deviation from its full meaning, an exaggeration and a loss of insight. Because poetry may influence politics we conclude that poetry is merely politics, or a kind of addlepated politics, and thus not good for anything. Why this has come about there is not time to say here, even if I knew. One may point out some of the ways in which it has affected our general views, and hence see how it works in us.

How does it happen that literary men themselves blame the poets first when society goes wrong? The argument we heard ten years ago runs somewhat as follows: The rise of Hitlerism (we were not then looking too narrowly at Stalinism) reflects the failure of our age to defend the principles of social and political democracy, a failure resulting from the apathy of responsible classes of society, those persons who have charge of the means of public influence that was formerly called language (but is now called "communications"). These persons are the writers, more particularly the poets or "makers," whose special charge is the purity of language and who represent the class of writers presumably at its highest. The makers, early in the nineteenth century, retired to a private world of their own invention, where they cultivated certain delusions—for example, their superiority to practical life, the belief in the autonomy of poetry, and the worship of the past. Some of them, like Baudelaire, actively disliked democracy. Their legacy to our tortured age turned out to be at once the wide diffusion and the intensification of these beliefs, with the result that we became politically impotent, and totalitarianism went unchecked.

This argument is impressive and we cannot wholly dismiss it; for directed somewhat differently it points to a true state of affairs: there was a moral and political apathy in the western countries, and there was no decisive stand against Nazism until it was too late to prevent war. Did the men of letters, the "clerks," have a monopoly upon this apathy? We may answer this question from two points of view. First, is there anything in the nature of poetry, as it has been sung or written in many different kinds of societies, which would justify putting so great a burden of *general* responsibility upon the man of imagination? Secondly, was there no other class of "intellectuals" in the modern world, scientists, philosophers, or statesmen, who might also be called into account?

If we address ourselves to the second question first, we shall have to observe that philosophers, scientists, and politicians have by and large assumed that they had no special responsibility for the chaos of the modern world. Mr. Einstein not long ago warned us that we now have the power to destroy ourselves. There was in his statement no reference to his own great and perhaps crucial share in the scientific progress which had made the holocaust possible. If it occurs, will Mr. Einstein be partly to blame, provided there is anybody left to blame him? Will God hold him responsible? I shall not try to answer that question. And I for one should not be willing to take the responsibility, if I had the capacity, of settling the ancient question of how much natural knowledge should be placed in the hands of men whose moral and spiritual education has not been impressive: by such men I mean the majority at all times and places, and more particularly the organized adolescents of all societies known as the military class.

Here we could meditate upon (or if we like better to do it, pray over) the spectacle, not military, widely reported in the newspapers, of the President of Harvard University congratulating his colleagues with evident delight when the first atom bomb was exploded in the desert. Among those present at Los Alamos on July 14, 1945, at five-thirty in the morning, were Mr. Conant and Mr. Bush. "On the instant that all was over," reported the New York *Times,* "these men leaped to their feet, the terrible tension ended, they shook hands, embraced each other and shouted in delight." We have no right to explore another man's feelings, or to say what should please him. Nobody then or since has said that Mr. Conant's emotions, whatever they may have been on that occasion, were irresponsible. Nor do I wish to use Mr. Conant or any other scientist, or administrator of the sciences, as a whipping-boy for his colleagues. Yet it is a fact that we cannot blink, that the Renaissance doctrine of the freedom of unlimited equiry has had consequences for good and evil in the modern world. This doctrine has created our world; in so far as we are able to enjoy it we must credit unlimited enquiry with its material benefits. But its dangers are too notorious to need pointing out. An elusive *mystique* supports the general doctrine, which may be stated as follows: We must keep up the enquiry, come hell and high water.

One way to deal with this modern demi-religion is to say that a part of its "truth" must be suppressed. I am not ready to say that: I am only ready to point out that it is not suppression of *truth* to decline to commit wholesale slaughter even if we have the means of committing it beyond the reach of any known technique of the past. Is it suppression of truth to withhold from general use the means of exploiting a technique of slaughter? How might it be withheld, should we agree that it is both desirable and possible to do so? If we let government suppress it, government will in the long run suppress everything and everybody else—even democratic government. There is no just way of holding individuals and classes responsible for the moral temper of an entire civilization.

At this point the theologians and humanists, the men of God and the men of man, appear—or at any rate formerly appeared. The Christian religion, in its various sects, has been blamed for its historic conservatism in refusing to sanction the advances of science as they were made. It is my impression that this supposedly Christian scepticism is Arabic in origin. It was the followers of Averroës in Europe who upheld the secret cult of natural knowledge against the Thomists and the Scotists, who more than the disciples of Roger Bacon stood for the diffusion of scientific enquiry. It is significant that the one science of the ancient world that impinged directly upon the daily lives of men—medicine—was held to be esoteric; the school of Hippocrates hid the secrets of the "art" lest the uninitiate abuse them and pervert them to the uses of witchcraft. This is not the place, and I am not competent enough, to follow up this line of speculation. I have wished only to observe that before the Christian dispensation, and well into it, the professors of special knowledge tried to be responsible for the public use of their techniques. We have not, so far as I know, a record of any of their reasons for what we should consider an illiberal suppression of truth. But if we think of the Greek world of thought as having lasted about nine hundred years, down to the great pupils of Plotinus—Iamblichus and Porphyrius—we may see in it a sense of the whole of life which must not be too quickly disturbed for the prosecution of special scientific interests. Nature was investigated, but it was a nature whose destiny in relation to a transcendental order was already understood. The classical insight into this relation was, as usual, recorded very early in a myth—that of the brothers Prometheus and Epimetheus—which now gives signs of recovering the authority which in the modern world it had yielded to myths that science had created about itself.

The responsibility of the scientist has not, I am sure, been defined by this digression: I have merely suggested that if anybody have a specific responsibility it may be the scientist himself. His myth of omnipotent rationality has worked certain wonders; but perhaps a little too rapidly. In Shelley's "Defense of Poetry" there is a sentence that persons who press the poet to legislate for us seldom quote: "Our calculations have outrun conception; we have eaten more than we can digest." Shall we hold the scientists responsible for this? Have they made the child sick on green apples? I do not say that they have. But the child is sick. If the scientist is not responsible, are philosophers, statesmen, and poets, particularly poets, responsible?

Before I return to the poet's responsibility, I shall consider briefly the possible responsibility of other persons, excluding this time the scientists, about whom it has become evident that I know little; and I can scarcely do more than allude to the other intellectual classes whose special disciplines might conceivably implicate them in care for the public good. Of the philosophers I likewise speak with neither information nor knowledge. Like Mr. Santayana, I might somewhat presumptuously describe myself as "an ignorant man, almost a poet." But one gets strongly the impression that the classical metaphysical question—What is the nature of Being?—is semantically meaningless in our age, a mere historicism reserved for the frivolous occasions of lecture-room philosophy. Our going philosophy is reported to me as a curious, apostolic activity known as the "philosophy of science," an attempt to devise a language for all the sciences which through it would arrive at "unity." This is no doubt a laudable program, unity being usually better than disunity, unless the things to be joined do not like each other, or, again, unless the union take place at a level of abstraction at which certain things become excluded, such as human nature, of which the Nazi and the Stalinist unities for some reason took little account. But these are unities of the political order. What have the philosophers of unified science to do with them? They glanced at them, I believe, in resolutions passed at philosophical congresses, or in interviews for the press, where we were told that things will continue to go badly until men behave more rationally. Rationality usually turned out to be liberalism, or the doctrine that reason, conceived in instrumental terms, will eventually perfect us, even though our situation may be getting worse every day. This, it seems to me, was the contribution of certain philosophers to the recent war. Was the contribution responsible or irresponsible? Common sense ought to tell us that it was neither; and common sense tells us that not all philosophers talked this way. Everybody knows that modern philosophers, like their brother scientists, and not unlike their distant cousins the poets, are pursuing specialisms of various kinds; and from the point of view of these interests, the investigation of the nature of being, with the attendant pursuit of the love of wisdom, is no more within their purview than it is within mine. In his extra-laboratory pronouncements the merged philosopher-scientist sounds uncomfortably like his famous creation in allegorical fiction, the "man in the street"—the man without specialisms who used to sit on the cracker barrel, and who, in all ages, since hats were invented, has talked through his hat. Perhaps it was neither responsible nor irresponsible: it was merely dull to use the prestige of the philosophy of science as the stump from which to deliver commonplaces that were already at your and my command, and that were doing us so little good that they might be suspected of having caused a part of our trouble. Reason—in the sense of moderate unbelief in difficult truths about human nature—and belief in the perfectibility of man-in-the-gross, were the great liberal dogmas which underlay much of our present trouble. The men in charge of nature never told me that I ought to try to perfect myself; that would be done for me by my not believing that I could do anything about it, by relying upon history to do it, by the invocation of ideals that many of us thought were democratic, by the resolutions of committees, conventions, and associations; and not least by condescending affirmations of faith in the Common Man, a fictitious person with whom neither the philosopher-scientist nor I had even a speaking acquaintance. Will it not be borne in upon us in the next few years that Hitler and Stalin *are* the Common Man, and that one of the tasks of democracy is to allow as many men as possible to make themselves uncommon?

Thus it is my impression that belief in a false liberal democracy was not lacking among certain classes of "intellectuals" in the period between the wars: the period, in fact, in which Mr. MacLeish and Mr. Brooks said that we had staggered into a war that might have been prevented had the men of letters not given us such a grim view of modern man from their ivory towers, or simply refused to be concerned about him. If the more respectable "intellectuals" were not heeded in the call to democratic action, would the mere literary men have been heeded? Was the poet's prestige so great that his loss of democratic faith (assuming he had lost it) set so bad an example that it offset the testimony to the faith of even the statesman?

By the statesman one means, of course, the politician, though one would like to mean more, whether he carry the umbrella or the infectious smile, the swastika or the hammer-and-sickle. It would seem to have been the specific duty of the politician to have kept the faith and forestalled the rise of Nazism, though it was not generally supposed that it was up to him to do anything about Soviet Russia, which was tacitly assumed, if not by you and me, then by the leaves in Vallombrosa, to be on our side. My own disappointment in the politician is somewhat mitigated by the excuse which his failure provides for the poet: if he could not baulk the enemy, whom he directly confronted, what chance had the poet?—the poet, whose best weapon in history seems to have been Shelley's fleet of toy boats, each bearing a cargo of tracts, which he committed to the waters of Hyde Park.

I am sorry to sound frivolous; I confess that the political responsibility of poets bores me; I am discussing it because it irritates me more than it bores me. It irritates me because the poet has a great responsibility of his own: it is the responsibility to be a poet, to write poems, and not to gad about using the rumor of his verse, as I am now doing, as the excuse to appear on platforms and to view with alarm. I have a deep, unbecoming suspicion of such talking poets: whatever other desirable things they may believe in, they do not believe in poetry. They believe that poets should write tracts, or perhaps autobiographies; encourage the public, further this cause or that, good or bad, depending upon whose political ox is being gored.

My own political ox was at least driven into a fence-corner when Mr. Pound thumped his tub for the Axis; but what I cannot easily forgive him was thumping any tub at all—unless, as a private citizen, dissociated from the poet, he had decided to take political action at some modest level, such as giving his life for his country, where whatever he did would be as inconspicuous as his ejaculatory political philosophy demanded that it be. But on Radio Rome he appeared as Professor Ezra Pound, the great American Poet. Much the same can be said of Mr. MacLeish himself. It is irrelevant that I find his political principles (I distinguish his *principles* from his *views*), in so far as I understand them, more congenial than Mr. Pound's. The immediate *views* of these poets seem to me equally hortatory, quasi-lyrical, and ill-grounded. We might imagine for them a pleasant voyage in one of Percy Shelley's boats. If society indicted and condemned poets for the mixture and the misuse of two great modes of action, poetry and politics, we might have to indict Mr. Pound a second time, as it could conceivably be done in some Swiftian social order; and we should have in fairness to provide an adjoining cell for Mr. MacLeish.

The relation of poetry and of other high imaginative literature to social action was not sufficiently considered in the attacks and counter-attacks of the past ten years. No one knows precisely what the relation is; so I shall not try here to define it; though what I am about to say will imply certain assumptions. There is no doubt that poetry, even that of Mallarmé, has some effect upon conduct, in so far as it affects our emotions. To what extent is the poetry itself, even that of Mallarmé, an effect? The total complex of sensibility and thought, of belief and experience, in the

TO WHOM IS THE POET RESPONSIBLE?

ing factor that the poet must first of all be aware of; otherwise his language will lack primary reality, the nexus of
thing and word. The failure to consider this primary reality produces willed poetry which usually ignores the
human condition. The human condition must be faced and
embodied in language before men in any age can envisage
the possibility of action. To suggest that poets tell men in
crisis what to do, to insist that *as poets* they acknowledge
themselves as legislators of the social order, is to ask them
to shirk their specific responsibility, which is quite simply
the reality of man's experience, not what his experience
ought to be, in any age. *To whom* is the poet responsible?
He is responsible to his *conscience,* in the French sense of
the word: the joint action of knowledge and judgment.
This conscience has long known a severe tradition of propriety in discerning the poet's particular kind of actuality.
No crisis, however dire, should be allowed to convince us
that the relation of the poet to his permanent reality can
ever change. And thus the poet is not responsible to
society for a version of what it thinks it is or what it wants.
For what is the poet responsible? He is responsible for the
virtue proper to him as poet, for his special *arête*: for the
mastery of a disciplined language which will not shun the
full report of the reality conveyed to him by his awareness: he must hold, in Yeats' great phrase, "reality and
justice in a single thought."

We have virtually turned the argument of the attack
around upon itself. For it was an irresponsible demand to
ask the poet to cease to be a poet and become the propa-
gandist of a political ideal, even if he himself thought it a
worthy ideal. If the report of the imagination on the real-
ities of western culture in the past century was as de-
pressing as the liberal mind said it was, would not the

[29]

scientist, the philosopher, and the statesman have done well to study it? They might have got a clue to what was wrong. They were, I believe, studying graphs, charts, and "trends"—the indexes of power—but not human nature. The decay of modern society is nowhere more conspicuous than in the loss of the arts of reading on the part of men of action. It was said at the beginning of the war that the traditions of modern literature represented by Proust had powerfully contributed to the collapse of Europe. It was not supposed that the collapse of Europe might have affected those traditions. If the politicians had been able to read Proust, or Joyce, or even Kafka, might they not have discerned more sharply what the trouble was, and done something to avert the collapse? I doubt it; but it makes as much sense as the argument that literature can be a cause of social decay. If, for example, Mr. Churchill had been able to quote the passage about Ciacco from the *Inferno*, or the second part of *The Waste Land*, instead of Arthur Hugh Clough, might we have hoped that men would now be closer to the reality out of which sound political aspiration must arise?

I leave this subject with the observation that poetry had to be attacked for not having done all that men had expected of it at the end of the nineteenth century. "The future of poetry is immense," said Matthew Arnold. It had to be immense because, for men like Arnold, everything else had failed. It was the new religion that was destined to be lost more quickly than the old. Poetry was to have saved us; it not only hadn't saved us by the end of the fourth decade of this century; it had only continued to be poetry which was little read. It had to be rejected. The primitive Athenians, at the Thargelian festival of Apollo, killed two human beings, burnt them, and cast their ashes into the sea. The men sacrificed were called

TO WHOM IS THE POET RESPONSIBLE?

pharmakoi: medicines. We have seen in our time a powerful attempt to purify ourselves of the knowledge of evil in man. Poetry is one of the sources of that knowledge. It is believed by some classical scholars that the savage ritual of the *pharmakoi* was brought to Athens by Barbarians. In historical times effigies made of dough were substituted for human beings.

3

The Symbolic Imagination[1]

The Mirrors of Dante

IT IS RIGHT even if it is not quite proper to observe at the beginning of a discourse on Dante, that no writer has held in mind at one time the whole of *The Divine Comedy*: not even Dante, perhaps least of all Dante himself. If Dante and his Dantisti have not been equal to the view of the whole, a view shorter than theirs must be expected of the amateur who, as a writer of verses, vainly seeks absolution from the mortal sin of using poets for what he can get out of them. I expect to look at a single image in the *Paradiso*, and to glance at some of its configurations with other images. I mean the imagery of light, but I mean chiefly its reflections. It was scarcely necessary for Dante to have read, though he did read, the *De Anima*, to learn that sight is the king of the senses and that the human body, which like other organisms lives by *touch*, may be

1. This essay and "The Angelic Imagination" which follows it were given in shorter versions as the Candlemas Lectures at Boston College, February 10–11, 1951.

made actual in language only through the imitation of *sight*. And sight in language is imitated not by means of "description"—*ut pictura poesis*—but by doubling the image: our confidence in its spatial reality is won quite simply by casting the image upon a glass, or otherwise by the insinuation of space between.

I cannot undertake to examine here Dante's double imagery in all its detail, for his light alone could lead us into complexities as rich as life itself. I had almost said richer than life, if by life we mean (as we must mean) what we ourselves are able daily to see, or even what certain writers have seen, with the exception of Shakespeare, and possibly of Sophocles and Henry James. A secondary purpose that I shall have in view will be to consider the dramatic implications of the light imagery as they emerge at the resolution of the poem, in Canto XXXIII of the *Paradiso*. These implications suggest, to my mind, a radical change in the interpretation of *The Divine Comedy*, and impel me to ask again: What kind of poem is it? In asking this question I shall not be concerned with what we ordinarily consider to be literary criticism; I shall be only incidentally judging, for my main purpose is to describe.

In *Purgatorio* XXX Beatrice appears to Dante first as a voice (what she says need not detain us here), then as light; but not yet the purest light. She is the light of a pair of eyes in which is reflected the image of the gryphon, a symbol of the hypostatic union, of which she herself is a "type." But before Dante perceives this image in her eyes, he says: "A thousand desires hotter than flame held my eyes bound to the shining eyes. . . ."[2] I see no reason to suppose that Dante does not mean what he says. *Mille*

2. Quotations in English from *The Divine Comedy* are from the translation by Carlyle, Okey, and Wicksteed, in the Temple Classics edition. Here and there I have taken the liberty of neutralizing certain victorian poeticisms, which were already archaic in that period.

[33]

disiri più che fiamma caldi I take to be the desires, however interfused by this time with courtly and mystical associations, of a man for a woman: the desires that the boy Dante felt for the girl Beatrice in 1274 after he had passed her in a street of Florence. She is the same Beatrice, Dante the same Dante, with differences which do not reject but rather include their sameness. Three dancing girls appear: Dante's allegory, formidable as it is, intensifies rather than impoverishes the reality of the dancers as girls. Their dance is a real dance, their song, in which they make a charming request of Beatrice, is a real song. If Dante expected us to be interested in the dancers only as the Theological Virtues, I see no good reason why he made them girls at all. They are sufficiently convincing as the Three Graces, and I cannot feel in the pun a serious violation of Dante's confidence. The request of the girls is sufficiently remarkable: *Volgi, Beatrice, volgi gli occhi santi*—"Turn, Beatrice, turn those holy eyes." Let Dante see your holy eyes; look into his eyes. Is it extravagant to substitute for the image of the gryphon the image of Dante in Beatrice's eyes? I think not. *He is in her eyes*—as later, in *Paradiso* XXXIII, he will be "in" God. Then a startling second request by the dancers: "Of thy grace do us the favor that thou unveil thy mouth to him"—*disvele / a lui la bocca tua* . . . "that he may discern the second beauty which thou hidest"—*la seconda belleza che tu cele.* At this point we get one of the innumerable proofs of Dante's greatness as a poet. We are not shown *la seconda belleza,* the smiling mouth; we are shown, instead, in the first four *terzine* of the next canto, the effect on Dante. For neither Dante nor Homer *describes* his heroine. As Beatrice's mouth is revealed, all Dante's senses but the sense of sight are *tutti spenti;* and sight itself is caught in *l'antica rete*—"the ancient net"—a variation of *l'antica fiamma*—"the ancient flame"—that he

[34]

had felt again when he had first seen Beatrice in the Earthly Paradise.

What the net is doing here seems now to me plain, after some ten years of obtuseness about it. The general meaning is, as Charles Williams holds, that Dante, having chosen the Way of Affirmation through the physical image, feels here in the Earthly Paradise all that he had *felt* before, along with what he now *knows*. Why did he put the worldly emotion of his youthful life into the figure of the net? It is not demanded by the moment; we should not have the sense of missing something if it were not there. If it is a simple metaphor for the obfuscation of sensuality, it is not a powerful metaphor; we must remember that Dante uses very few linguistic metaphors, as distinguished from analogical or symbolic objects; when he uses them they are simple and powerful. The net, as I see it, is not simply a metaphor for the "catching" of Dante by Beatrice in 1274, though it is partly *that* ancient net; it is also a net of even more famous antiquity, that in which Venus caught Mars; and it is thus a symbolic object. Moreover, if Beatrice's eyes are univocally divine, why do the three Theological Dancers reproach him with gazing at her "too fixedly"—*troppo fiso*—as if he or anybody else could get too much of the divine light? He is, of course, not yet ready for the full Beatific Vision. But an astonishing feature of the great scene of the divine pageant is that, as a trope, a subjective effect, the smile of Beatrice simultaneously revives his human love (Eros) and directs his will to the anticipation of the Beatific Vision (Agapé): both equally, by means of the action indicated by the blinding effect of both; he is blinded by the net and by the light, not alternately but at one instant.[3]

3. It seems scarcely necessary to remind the reader that I have followed in the scene of the Earthly Paradise only one thread of an immense number in a vastly complex pattern.

[35]

To bring together various meanings at a single moment of action is to exercise what I shall speak of here as the symbolic imagination; but the line of *action* must be unmistakable, we must never be in doubt about what is happening; for at a given stage of his progress the hero does one simple thing, and one only. The symbolic imagination conducts an action through analogy, of the human to the divine, of the natural to the supernatural, of the low to the high, of time to eternity. My literary generation was deeply impressed by Baudelaire's sonnet *Correspondances*, which restated the doctrines of medieval symbolism by way of Swedenborg; we were impressed because we had lost the historical perspective leading back to the original source. But the statement of a doctrine is very different from its possession as experience in poetry. Analogical symbolism need not move towards an act of imagination. It may see in active experience the qualities necessary for static symbolism; for example, the Grave of Jesus, which for the theologian may be a symbol to be expounded in the Illuminative Way, or for the mystic may be an object of contemplation in the Unitive Way. Despite the timeless orders of both rational discourse and intuitive contemplation, it is the business of the symbolic poet to return to the order of temporal sequence—to *action*. His purpose is to show men experiencing whatever they may be capable of, with as much meaning as he may be able to see in it; but the action comes first. Shall we call this the Poetic Way? It is at any rate the way of the poet, who has got to do his work with the body of this world, whatever that body may look like to him, in his time and place—the whirling atoms, the body of a beautiful woman, or a deformed body, or the body of Christ, or even the body of this death. If the poet is able to put into this moving body, or to find in it, a coherent chain of analogies, he will inform an intuitive act with symbolism; his will be in one degree or another the symbolic imagination.

Before I try to illustrate these general reflections, I must make a digression, for my own guidance, which I am not competent to develop as searchingly as my subject demands. The symbolic imagination takes rise from a definite limitation of human rationality which was recognized in the West until the 17th Century; in this view the intellect cannot have direct knowledge of essences. The only created mind that has this knowledge is the angelic mind.[4] If we do not believe in angels we shall have to invent them in order to explain by parable the remarkable appearance, in Europe, at about the end of the 16th Century, of a mentality which denied man's commitment to the physical world, and set itself up in quasi-divine independence. This mind has intellect and will without feeling; and it is through feeling alone that we witness the glory of our servitude to the natural world, to St. Thomas' accidents, or, if you will, to Locke's secondary qualities; it is our tie with the world of sense. The angelic mind suffers none of the limitations of sense; it has immediate knowledge of essences; and this knowledge moves through the perfect will to divine love, with which it is at one. Imagination in an angel is thus inconceivable, for the angelic mind transcends the mediation of both image and discourse. I call that human imagination angelic which tries to disintegrate or to circumvent the image in the illusory pursuit of essence. When human beings undertake this ambitious program, divine love becomes so rarefied that it loses its human paradigm, and is dissolved in the worship of intellectual power, the surrogate of divinity that worships itself.

4. The difficulties suffered by man as angel were known at least as early as Pascal; but the doctrine of angelism, as a force in the modern mind, has been fully set forth for the first time by Jacques Maritain in *The Dream of Descartes* (New York, 1944).

It professes to know nature as essence at the same time that it has become alienated from nature in the rejection of its material forms.

It was, however high the phrases [writes Charles Williams], the common thing from which Dante always started, as it was certainly the greatest and most common to which he came. His images were the natural inevitable images—the girl in the street, the people he knew, the language he learned as a child. In them the great diagrams were perceived; from them the great myths open; by them he understands the final end.[5]

This is the simple secret of Dante, but it is a secret which is not necessarily available to the Christian poet today. The Catholic faith has not changed since Dante's time. But the Catholic sensibility, as we see it in modern Catholic poetry, from Thompson to Lowell, has become angelic, and is not distinguishable (doctrinal differences aside) from poetry by Anglicans, Methodists, Presbyterians, and atheists. I take it that more than doctrine, even if the doctrine be true, is necessary for a great poetry of action. Catholic poets have lost, along with their heretical friends, the power to start with the "common thing": they have lost the gift for concrete experience. The abstraction of the modern mind has obscured their way into the natural order. Nature offers to the symbolic poet clearly denotable objects in depth and in the round, which yield the analogies to the higher syntheses. The modern poet rejects the higher synthesis, or tosses it in a vacuum of abstraction.[6] If he looks at nature he spreads the clear visual image in a complex of metaphor, from one katachresis to another through Aristotle's permutations of genus and species. He cannot

5. Charles Williams: *The Figure of Beatrice* (London, 1943), p. 44.
6. Another way of putting this is to say that the modern poet, like Valéry or Crane, tries to seize directly the anagogical meaning, without going through the three preparatory stages of letter, allegory, and trope.

sustain the prolonged analogy, the second and superior kind of figure that Aristotle doubtless had in mind when he spoke of metaphor as the key to the resemblances of things, and the mark of genius.

That the gift of analogy was not Dante's alone every medievalist knows. The most striking proof of its diffusion and the most useful example for my purpose that I know, is the letter of St. Catherine of Siena to Brother Raimondo of Capua. A young Sienese, Niccolo Tuldo, had been un-justly convicted of treason and condemned to death. Catherine became his angel of mercy, giving him daily solace— the meaning of the Cross, the healing powers of the Blood; and so reconciled him to the faith that he accepted his last end. Now I have difficulty believing people who say that they live in the Blood of Christ, for I take them to mean that they have the faith and hope some day to live in it. The evidence of the Blood is one's power to produce it, the power to show it as a "common thing" and to make it real, literally, in action. For the report of the Blood is very different from its reality. St. Catherine does not report it; she recreates it, so that its analogical meaning is confirmed again in blood that she has seen. This is how she does it:

Then [the condemned man] came, like a gentle lamb; and see-ing me he began to smile, and wanted me to make the sign of the Cross. When he had received the sign, I said, "Down! To the bridal, my sweetest brother. For soon shalt thou be in the enduring life." He prostrated himself with great gentleness, and I stretched out his neck; and bowed me down, and recalled to him the Blood of the Lamb. His lips said naught save Jesus! and Catherine! And so saying, I received his head in my hands, clos-ing my eyes in the divine goodness and saying, "I will."

When he was at rest my soul rested in peace and quiet, and in so great fragrance of blood that I could not bear to remove the blood which had fallen on me from him.

It is deeply shocking, as all proximate incarnations of the Word are shocking, whether in Christ and the Saints, or in Dostoevsky, James Joyce, or Henry James. I believe it was T. S. Eliot who made accessible again to an ignorant generation a common Christian insight, when he said that people cannot bear very much reality. I take this to mean that only persons of extraordinary courage, and perhaps even genius, can face the spiritual truth in its physical body. Flaubert said that the artist, the soldier, and the priest face death every day; so do we all; yet it is perhaps nearer to them than to other men; it is their particular responsibility. When St. Catherine "rests in so great fragrance of blood," it is no doubt the Blood of the Offertory which the celebrant offers to God *cum odore suavitatis,* but with the literal odor of the species of wine, not of blood. St. Catherine had the courage of genius which permitted her to *smell* the Blood of Christ in Niccolo Tuldo's blood clotted on her dress: she smelled the two bloods *not alternately but at one instant,* in a single act compounded of spiritual insight and physical perception.

Chekhov said that a gun hanging on the wall at the beginning of a story has got to be fired off before the story ends: everything in potency awaits its completed purpose in act. If this is a metaphysical principle, it is also the prime necessity of the creative imagination. Is not St. Catherine telling us that the Blood of Christ must be perpetually recreated as a brute fact? If the gun has got to be fired, the Blood has got to be shed, if only because that is the first condition of its appearance; it must move towards the condition of human action, where we may smell it, touch it, and taste it again.

When ecclesiastical censorship of this deep insight in the laity exceeds a just critical prudence, the result is not merely obscurantism in the arts; it is perhaps a covert rejection of the daily renewal of the religious life. Twenty-five years ago the late W. B. Yeats had a controversy with the Irish bishops about the famous medieval Cherry Tree Carol, which the hierarchy wished to suppress as blasphemous. The Blessed Virgin is resting under a cherry tree, too tired to reach up and pluck a cherry. Since Christ lives from the foundations of the world, He is omnipotent in the womb, and He commands the tree to lower a bough for His Mother's convenience; which it obligingly does, since it cannot do otherwise. Here again the gun is fired and the Blood is shed. If the modern Church has lost the historic experience of this kind of symbolism, which is more tolerable, I believe, in the Latin countries than with us, it is at least partial evidence that the Church has lost the great culture that it created, and that at intervals has created the life of the Church.

I return from this digression to repeat that Dante was the great master of the symbolism, the meaning of which I have been trying to suggest. But the symbolic "problem" of *The Divine Comedy* we must not suppose Dante to have undertaken analytically; it is our problem, not his. Dr. Flanders Dunbar has stated it with great penetration:

As with his progress he perceives more and more of ultimate reality through the symbol [Beatrice], at the same time the symbol occupies less and less of his attention, until ultimately it takes its place among all created things on a petal of the rose, while he gazes beyond it into the full glory of the sun.[7]

The symbolic problem, then, is: How shall Dante move step by step (literally and allegorically) from the Dark Wood, the negation of light, to the "three circles, of three colors and one magnitude," God Himself, or pure light, where there are no sensible forms to reflect it? There can

7. H. Flanders Dunbar: *Symbolism in Mediaeval Thought and Its Consummation in The Divine Comedy* (New Haven, 1929), p. 347.

be no symbol for God, for that which has itself informed step by step the symbolic progress. Vision, giving us clear visual objects, through physical sight, moving steadily upward towards its anagogical transfiguration, is the first matrix of the vast analogical structure. As Dante sees more he sees less: as he sees more light the nearer he comes to its source, the less he sees of what it had previously lit up. In the Empyrean, at the climax of the Illuminative Way, Beatrice leaves Dante and takes her place in the Rose; St. Bernard now guides him into the Intuitive Way.

For the Illuminative Way is the way to knowledge through the senses, by means of aided reason, but here the "distance" between us and what we see is always the distance between a concept and its object, between the human situation in which the concept arises and the realization of its full meaning. Put otherwise, with the beginning of the *Vita Nuova* in mind, it is the distance between the knowledge of love, which resulted from the earthly love of Dante for Beatrice, and the distant "object," or God, that had made the love in the first place possible: the distance between Beatrice and the light which had made it possible for him to see her. The Kantian synthetic proposition of the entire poem, as we enter it through the symbolism of light, is: Light is Beatrice. Here the eye is still on the human image; it is still on it up to the moment when she takes her place with the other saints in the Rose, where she is only one of many who turn their eyes to the "eternal fountain." Light is Beatrice; light is her *smile;* her final smile, which Dante sees as she enters the Rose, is no longer the mere predicate of a sentence, for there is now no distance between the smile and what had lit it. Although, in so far as it is a smile at all, it is still the smile at the unveiling of the mouth, it is now the smile without the mouth, the smile of light. And thus we arrive at the converse of the proposition: Beatrice is light. Now Dante's eye is on the light itself, but he cannot see it because Beatrice, through whose image he had progressively seen more light, has disappeared; and he can see nothing. There is nothing to *see*. For that which enables sight is not an object of vision. What has been seen is, in what is surely one of the greatest passages of all poetry, "the shadowy prefaces of their truth." Illumination, or intellect guided by divine grace, powerful as it is, halts at the "prefaces." But the Unitive Way leads to the Presence, where both sight and discursive thought cease.

Whether Dante should have tried to give us an image of God, of that which is without image and invisible, is an unanswerable question. Is it possible that we have here a break in the symbolic structure, which up to the end of the poem has been committed to the visible? At the end we are with Love, whose unpredicated attribute is the entire universe. Has Dante given us, in the "three circles, of three colors and one magnitude," merely the trinitarian and doctrinal equivalent of the ultimate experience, instead of an objective symbol of the experience itself? In the terms of Dante's given structure, such a symbol was perhaps not possible; and strictly speaking it is never possible. If he was going to give us anything he doubtless had to give us just what he gave; he gave it in an act of great artistic heroism. For in the center of the circles he sees the image of man. This is the risk, magnified almost beyond conception, of St. Catherine: the return of the suprarational and supra-sensible to the "common thing." It is the courage to see again, even in its ultimate cause, the Incarnation.

If we will look closely at the last four lines of the *Paradiso*, and double back on our tracks, I believe that we will see that there is no break in the *dramatic* structure—the structure of the action.[8] For the poem is an action: a man is acting and going somewhere, and things are happening both to him and around him; otherwise the poem would be—what I may have given the impression of its being— a symbolic machine. In the space of an essay I cannot prepare properly the background of the suggestion that I am about to offer. For one thing, we should have to decide who "Dante" is, and where he is in the action that he has depicted—questions that nobody seems to know much about. For what it may be worth, I suggest that the poet has undertaken to involve a fictional character named Dante —at once the poet and not the poet of that name—in a certain action of the greatest possible magnitude, the issue of which is nothing less, perhaps something greater, than life or death. In this action the hero fails. He fails in the sense that he will have to start over again when he steps out of the "poem," as he surely must do if he is going to write it.

Thus I see *The Divine Comedy* as essentially dramatic and, in one of its modes, tragic. Are we to suppose that the hero actually attained to the Beatific Vision? No; for nobody who had would be so foolish as to write a poem about it, if in that spiritual perfection it could even occur to him to do so. The poem is a vast paradigm of the possibility of the Beatific Vision. No more than its possibility for the individual person, for "Dante" himself, is here entertained. What shall we make of his failure of memory, the slipping away of the final image, which he calls *tanto oltraggio*— "so great an outrage?" It would be a nice question to decide whether something had slipped away, or whether it had ever been fully there. The vision is imagined, it is *imaged;*

8. By "dramatic" I mean something like *practic*, a possible adjective from *praxis*, a general movement of action as potency which it is the purpose of the poem to actualize. In the Thomist sequence, *potentia:actio: actus*, "dramatic" would roughly correspond to the middle term.

its essence is not possessed. I confess that it is not an argument from the poem to say that had Dante claimed its possession, he would have lost that "good of the intellect" which we forfeit when we presume to angelic knowledge; and it was through the good of the intellect that he was able to write the poem. But it is an external argument that I believe cannot be entirely ignored.

The last *terzina* of the last canto tells us: *All' alta fantasia qui mancò possa*—"To the high fantasy here power failed." What power failed? The power to write the poem, or the power to possess as experience the divine essence? Is it a literary or a religious failure? It is obviously and honorably both. It makes no more sense to say Dante achieved his final vision as direct experience than to say that Sophocles married his mother and put out his own eyes; that the experience of the *Oedipus Rex* represents the personal experience of Sophocles. What Dante achieved is an *actual* insight into the great dilemma, eternal life or eternal death, but he has not hedged the dilemma like a bet to warrant himself a favorable issue. As the poem closes, he still faces it, like the rest of us. Like Oedipus, the fictional Dante learns in humility a certain discipline of the will: we may equate up to a point the dark-blindness of Oedipus and the final light-blindness of Dante; both men have succeeded through suffering in blinding themselves to knowledge-through-sense, in the submission of *hybris* to a higher will.[9] The fictional Dante at the end steps out of the frame and becomes again the historical Dante; Oedipus steps out of his frame, his fictional plot is done, he is back in the world of unformed action, blind and, like Dante, an exile. Shall Oedipus be saved? Shall Dante? We do not know, but to ask the question is to point to a primary consideration in

9. Oedipus does not achieve this of course until the end of *Oedipus at Colonus*.

the interpretation of *The Divine Comedy*, particularly if we are disposed, as some commentators have been, to believe that Dante the man used his poem arrogantly to predict his own salvation.

If Dante does not wholly succeed in giving us in the "three circles, of three colors and one magnitude," an image of the Godhead, I think we are ready to see that it was not necessary; it was not a part of his purpose. Such an image is not the "final cause" of the poem. The poem is an action; it is an action to the end. For the image that Dante gives us of the Godhead is not an image to be received by the reader as essential knowledge in his own "angelic" intelligence, as an absolute apart from the action. It is a dramatic image; the image is of the action and the action is Dante's. To read Canto XXXIII in any other way would be perhaps to commit the blunder that M. Gilson warns us against: the blunder of thinking that Dante was writing a super-philosophical tract, or a pious embellishment of the doctrines of Thomas Aquinas, instead of a poem. The question, then, is not what is the right anagogical symbol for God; it is rather what symbol for God will serve tropologically (that is, morally and dramatically) for the tragic insight of the poet who knows, through the stages of the Three Ways, that the Beatific Vision is possible but uncertain of realization. Dante sees himself, Man, in the Triune Circles, and he is in the Seraphic Heaven of Love. But at the end desire and will are like a "wheel moving equally"; motion imparted to it at one point turns it as a whole, but it has to be moved, as the wheel of our own desire and will must be moved, by a force outside it. The wheel is Dante's last symbol of the great failure. Since it must be moved, it is not yet at one, not yet in unity, with the divine will; it obeys it, as those other wheels, the sun and stars, moved by love, obey.

I take it that the wheel is the final geometrical projection of the *visual* matrix of analogy; it is what the eye sees, the material form, and what in its anagoge it eventually aspires to become. We must remember that Beatrice's eyes are spheres, no less than the physical universe itself, which is composed of concentric spheres. The first circles that Dante shows us are in Canto III of the *Inferno*, Charon's— "for round his eyes were wheels of flame." The last, the Triune Circles, are the anagoge of the visual circle, and are without extension; they are pure light, the abstraction or sublimation of flame. Flame burning in a circle and light lighting up a circle, and what it encloses, are the prime sensible symbols of the poem. Only Satan, at the geometrical center of the world, occupies a point that cannot be located on any existing arc of the cosmos. This is the spherical (or circular) expression of Satan's absolute privation of light-as-love which in the Empyrean turns the will-wheel of Dante with the cosmic spheres. These are the will of God as love; and if we ignore the dramatic structure, and fail to look closely at the symbolic, we shall conclude that Dante is at one with the purpose of the universe. But, as we have seen, the symbolic structure is complicated by the action, and in the end the action prevails. That is to say, Dante is *still moving*. Everything that moves, says Dante the Thomist in his letter to Can Grande, has some imperfection in it because it is, in the inverse degree of its rate of motion, removed from the Unmoved Mover, the Triune Circles, God. By a twist of this argument, which, of course, as I shall presently indicate, is specious, Satan himself has no imperfection: he too lies immobile—except for the fanning wings that freeze the immobile damned in Giudecca —as the Still Point in the Triune Circles is immobile. If Dante's will is turning like a wheel, he is neither damned nor saved; he is morally active in the universal human predicament. His participation in the love imparted as motion to the universe draws him towards the Triune Circles and to the immobility of peace at the center, as it draws all creatures; but a defection of the will could plunge him into the other "center."

Now Dante is astonished when he sees in the Primum Mobile a reversal of the ratio of speed of the spheres as he had observed it on earth, through the senses. "But in the universe of sense," he says to Beatrice, "we may see the circlings more divine as from the center they are more removed." In the spiritual universe the circlings are more divine the nearer they are to the center. It is a matter of perspective; from the earth outward the revolutions of the spheres are increasingly rapid up to the ninth, the Primum Mobile, whose speed is just short of infinite; the Primum Mobile is trying to achieve with all points of its surface a simultaneous contact with the Still Point of the Empyrean. What he sees in the Primum Mobile is this perspective visually reversed; instead of being the outer "crust" of the universe, the Primum Mobile is actually next to the central Still Point, whirling with inconceivable speed. God, the Still Point, is a non-spatial entity which is *everywhere* and *nowhere*. The Ptolemaic cosmos, which had been Christianized by the imposition of the angelic hierarchy of Dionysius, has been, in a way not to be completely visualized, turned inside out. The spheres, which began their career as an astronomical hypothesis, are now no longer necessary; they are replaced in the ultimate reality by nine non-spatial gradations of angelic intelligence, in three triads, the last and ninth circle of "fire" being that of the simple angels, the "farthest" removed in the non-spatial continuum from the Divine Love.

Where then is the earth, with Satan at its exact center? I think we must answer: Where it has always been. But "where" that is we had better not try to say. At any rate neither Satan nor the earth is at the spiritual center. His immobility thus has no perfection. In the full spiritual reality, of which the center of the material universe becomes an outermost "rind," beyond space, Satan does not exist: he exists in the world of sense and in the human will. The darkness of hell, from the point of view of God (if I may be allowed the expression), is not an inner darkness, but an outer. So, in the progress from hell to the Empyrean, Dante has come from the inner darkness of man to the inner light of God; from the outer darkness of God to the outer light of man.

This anagogical conversion of symbol that I have been trying to follow in one of its threads is nowhere by Dante merely *asserted;* it is constantly moving, rendered moment by moment as *action.* Like most good poets, great or minor, Dante wrote better than he had meant to do; for if we took him at his word, in the letter to Can Grande, we should conclude that the *Paradiso* is a work of rhetoric calculated "to remove those living in this life from a state of misery and to guide them to a state of happiness." It seems probable that persons now enrolled among the Blessed got there without being compelled to see on the way all that Dante saw. Were we reading the poem for that kind of instruction, and knew not where else to find it, we might conclude that Dante's *luce intellectual,* with its transformations in the fourfold system of interpretation, is too great a price to pay even for salvation; or, at any rate, for most of us, the wrong price. It would perhaps be a mistake for a man to decide that he has become a Christian at the instance of Dante, unless he is prepared to see all that Dante saw—which is one thing, but always seen in at least two ways.

A clue to two of the ways is the mirror symbol. As we approach it, the kind of warning that Dante at intervals pauses to give us is not out of place. For if the way up to now has been rough, we may expect it from now on to be even rougher. The number of persons, objects, and places in *The Divine Comedy* that are reflections, replicas, or manifestations of things more remote is beyond calculation. The entire natural world is a replica *in reverse* of the supernatural world. That, I believe, we have seen so far only on the dubious authority of my own assertion. But if Dante is a poet (I agree with M. Gilson that he is) he will not be satisfied with assertion as such, even with the authority of the Church to support it. The single authority of poetry is a difficult criterion of actuality that must always remain beyond our reach. And in some sense of this actuality Dante has got to place his vast two-way analogy (heaven like the world, the world like heaven) on the scene of action, and make it move. Let us take the stance of Dante at the beginning of *Paradiso* XXVIII, and try to suggest some of the ways in which he moves it:

as in the mirror a taper's flame, kindled behind a man, is seen by
    him before it be in his sight or thought,
as he turns back to see whether the glass speak truth to him,
    and sees that it accords with it as song-words to the music;
so my memory recalls that I did turn, gazing upon the lovely
    eyes whence love had made the noose to capture me;
and when I turned, and my own eyes were struck by what appears in that orb whenever upon its circling the eye is
    well fixed,
a point I saw which rayed forth light so keen that all the vision
    that it flames upon must close because of its sharp point.

(One observes in passing that even in the Primum Mobile Beatrice bears the net-noose dimension of meaning.) Beatrice's eyes are a mirror in which is reflected that "sharp point," to which Dante, still at a distance from it, now turns his direct gaze. As he looks at it he sees for the first time what its reflection in Beatrice's eyes could not convey: that it is the sensible world turned inside out. For the sensible world as well as her eyes is only a reflection of the light from the sharp point. Now he is looking at the thing-in-itself. *He has at last turned away from the mirror which is the world.* What happens when we turn away from a mirror to look directly at the object which we saw reflected? I must anticipate Beatrice's famous experiment with one of my own. If you will place upon a table a box open at one end, the open end towards a mirror, and then look into the mirror, you will see the open end. Turn from the mirror and look at the box itself. You still see the open end, and thus you see the object *reversed.* If the box were reproduced, in the sense of being continued or moved *into* the mirror, the actual box would present, when we turn to it, a closed end; for the box and its reflection would show their respectively corresponding sides in congruent projection. Quantitative visualization of the cosmic reversal is not completely possible. But through the mirror analogy Dante performs a stupendous feat of the imagination that in kind has probably not been rivalled by any other poet. And it is an analogy that has been firmly grounded in action.

In conclusion I shall try to point to its literal base; for we have seen it, in *Paradiso* XXVIII, only as a simile; and if we had not had it laid down earlier as a physical fact to which we must assent, a self-contained phenomenon of the natural order, it would no doubt lack at the end that fullness of actuality which we do not wholly understand, but which we require of poetry. The self-contained fact of the natural order is established in Canto II of the *Paradiso*, where Beatrice performs a physical experiment. Some scholars have been moved by it to admire Dante for this single ray of positivistic enlightenment feebly glowing in the mind of a medieval poet. So far as I know, our critics

have not considered it necessary to be sufficiently unen-
lightened to see that Beatrice's experiment is merely
poetry.

Before I reproduce it I shall exhibit a few more examples
of the mirror symbol that appear at intervals in the five
last cantos. In Canto XXIX, 25-27, form permeates matter "as in glass . . . a ray so glows that from its coming
to its pervading all, there is no interval." Still in XXIX, 142-
145, at the end: "See now the height and breadth of the
eternal worth, since it has made itself so many mirrors
in which it is reflected, remaining in itself one as before."
At line 37 of Canto XXX we enter the Empyrean where
Dante sees the great River of Light "issuing its living
sparks"; it too is a mirror, for Beatrice explains: "The river
and the topaz gems that enter and go forth, and the smiling
grasses are prefaces of their truth" (i.e., of what they reflect). In Canto XXX, 85-87, Dante bends down to the
waves "to make mirrors of my eyes"; and again in XXX he
sees the Rose of Paradise, another mirror, in one of his
great similes:

And as a hillside reflects itself in water at its foot, as if to look
    upon its own adornment, when it is rich in grasses and in
    flowers,
so, mounting in the light, around, around, casting reflection in
    more than a thousand ranks I saw all that of us have won
    return up yonder.

And finally the climactic reflection, the "telic principle"
and the archetype of them all, in Canto XXX, 127-132:

The circling that in thee [in the Triune God] appeared to be
    conceived as a reflected light, by my eyes scanned a little,
in itself, of its own color, seemed to be painted with our effigy,
    and thereat my sight was all committed to it.

Where have these mirrors, which do their poetic work, the work of making the supra-sensible visible—one of the tasks of all poetry—where have they come from? The remote frame is doubtless the circular or spherical shape of the Ptolemaic cosmos;[10] but if there is glass in the circular frame, it reflects nothing until Virgil has left Dante to Beatrice's guidance in the Earthly Paradise (*Purgatorio* XXXI); where we have already glanced at the unveiling of mouth and eyes. I suggest that Beatrice's eyes in *Purgatorio* XXXI are the first mirror. But the image is not, at this early stage of Beatrice, sufficiently developed to bear all the strain of analogical weight that Dante intends to put upon it. For that purpose the mirror must be established as a literal mirror, a plain mirror, a "common thing."

He not only begins with the common thing; he continues with it, until at the end we come by disarming stages to a scene that no man has ever looked upon before. Every detail of Paradise is a common thing; it is the cumulative combination and recombination of natural objects beyond their "natural" relations, which staggers the imagination. "Not," says Beatrice to Dante, "that such things are in themselves harsh; but on your side is the defect, in that your sight is not yet raised so high."

A mirror is an artifact of the practical intellect, and as such can be explained by natural law: but there is no natural law which explains man as a mirror reflecting the image of God. The great leap is made in the interval between Canto II and Canto XXXIII of the *Paradiso*.

Dante, in Canto II, is baffled by the spots on the moon, supposing them to be due to alternating density and rarity of matter. No, says Beatrice in effect, this would be mon-

10. The popular "visual" translation of Aristotle's primary Unmoved Mover producing, *through being loved*, the primary cosmic motion, which is circular. The philosophical source of this idea, Book XII, Chapter 7, of the *Metaphysics*, Dante of course knew.

ism, a materialistic explanation of the diffusion of the divine light. The true explanation is very different: all saved souls are equally saved, and all the heavenly spheres are equally in heaven; but the divine light reaches the remoter spheres and souls according to the spiritual gifts of which they were capable in the natural world. "This is the formal principle," Beatrice says, summing up, "which produces, in conformity to the excellence of the object, the turbid and the clear."

Meanwhile she has asked Dante to consider a physical experiment to illustrate the unequal reception of the divine substance. Take three mirrors, she says, and set two of them side by side, and a third in the middle but farther back. Place a candle behind you, and observe its image reflected in each of the three mirrors. The middle reflection will be smaller but not less bright than the two others: "smaller" stands quantitatively for unequal reception of a quality, spiritual insight; "not less bright" likewise for equality of salvation. But what concerns us is a certain value of the experiment that Dante, I surmise, with the cunning of a great poet, slyly refuses to consider: the dramatic value of the experiment.

There are *three*[11] mirrors each reflecting the *one* light. In the heart of the Empyrean, as we have seen, Dante says:

In the profound and shining being of the deep light appeared to me *three* circles, of *three* colors and one magnitude.

In the middle is the effigy of man. The physical image of Dante had necessarily been reflected in each of the three mirrors of Canto II; but he had not seen it. I suggest that he was not then ready to see it; his dramatic (i.e., tropological) development fell short of the final self-knowledge.

11. Only two, placed at unequal distances from the candle, are strictly necessary for the experiment; but three are necessary as pointers towards the anagoge of the Trinity in the Triune Circles.

Self-knowledge comes to him, as an Aristotelian Recognition and Reversal, when he turns the cosmos inside out by turning away from the "real" mirrors to the one light which has cast the three separate images. For the first time he sees the "one magnitude," the candle itself. And it is all done with the simple apparatus and in conditions laid down in Canto II; he achieves the final anagoge and the dramatic recognition by turning around, as if he were still in Canto II, and by looking at the candle that has been burning all the time behind his back.

I have described some motions of the symbolic imagination in Dante, and tried to develop a larger motion in one of its narrower aspects. What I have left out of this discussion is very nearly the entire poem. In the long run the light-imagery is not the body, it is what permits us to *see* the body, of the poem. The rash suggestion that *The Divine Comedy* has a tragic mode—among other modes—I shall no doubt be made to regret; I cannot defend it further here. Perhaps the symbolic imagination is tragic in sentiment, if not always in form, in the degree of its development. Its every gain beyond the simple realism of experience imposes so great a strain upon any actuality of form as to set the ultimate limit of the gain as a defeat. The high order of the poetic insight that the final insight must elude us, is dramatic in the sense that its fullest image is an action in the shapes of this world: it does not reject, it includes; it sees not only with but through the natural world, to what may lie beyond it. Its humility is witnessed by its modesty. It never begins at the top; it carries the bottom along with it, however high it may climb.

4

The Angelic Imagination

Poe as God

WITH SOME EMBARRASSMENT I assume the part of amateur theologian and turn to a little-known figure, Edgar Allan Poe, another theologian only less ignorant than myself. How seriously one must take either Poe or his present critic in this new role I prefer not to be qualified to say. Poe will remain a man of letters—I had almost said a poet—whose interest for us is in the best sense historical. He represents that part of our experience which we are least able to face up to: the Dark Night of Sense, the cloud hovering over that edge of the eye which is turned to receive the effluvia of France, whence the literary power of his influence reaches us today. In France, the literary power has been closely studied; I shall not try to estimate it here. Poe's other power, that of the melancholy, heroic life, one must likewise leave to others, those of one's own compatriots who are not interested in literature. All readers of Poe, of the work or of the life, and the rare reader of both, are peculiarly liable to the vanity of discovery. I shall be concerned in the ensuing remarks with what I think I have seen in Poe that nobody else has seen:

this undetected quality, or its remote source in Poe's feeling and thought, I believe partly explains an engagement with him that men on both sides of the Atlantic have acknowledged for more than a century.

It was recently acknowledged, with reservations, by Mr. T. S. Eliot, whose estimate must be reckoned with: Poe, he tells us, won a great reputation in Europe because the continental critics habitually view an author's work as a whole; whereas English and American critics view each work separately and, in the case of Poe, have been stopped by its defects. Mr. Eliot's essay[1] is the first attempt by an English-speaking critic to bring to Poe the continental approach and to form a general estimate. I quote from what I take to be Mr. Eliot's summary; Poe, he says,

appears to yield himself completely to the idea of the moment: the effect is, that all his ideas seem to be entertained rather than believed. What is lacking is not brain-power, but that maturity of intellect which comes only with the maturing of the man as a whole, the development and coordination of the various emotions.

What I shall say towards the end of this essay I believe will show that Mr. Eliot is partly wrong, but that on the whole his estimate of Poe's immaturity is right. Does Poe merely "entertain" *all* his ideas? Perhaps all but one; but that one makes all the difference. Its special difference consists in his failure to see what the idea really was, so that he had perpetually to shift his ground—to "entertain," one after another, shabby rhetorics and fantasies that could never quite contain the one great idea. He was a religious man whose Christianity, for reasons that nobody knows anything about, had got short-circuited; he lived among fragments of provincial theologies, in the midst of which "co-

1. *From Poe to Valéry* (New York, 1949).

ordination," for a man of his intensity, was difficult if not impossible. There is no evidence that Poe used the word coordination in the sense in which Mr. Eliot finds him deficient in it; but it is justly applied. I am nevertheless surprised that Mr. Eliot seems to assume that *coordination* of the "various emotions" is ever possible: the word gives the case away to Poe. It is a morally neutral term that Poe himself might have used, in his lifelong effort to impose upon experience a mechanical logic; possibly it came into modern literary psychology from analytic geometry. I take it that the word was not used, if in Mr. Eliot's sense it was known, when considerable numbers of persons were able to experience coordination. I suppose Mr. Eliot means by it a harmony of faculties among different orders of experience; and Poe's failure to harmonize himself cannot be denied.

The failure resulted in a hypertrophy of the three classical faculties: feeling, will and intellect. The first I have discussed elsewhere.[2] It is the incapacity to represent the human condition in the central tradition of natural feeling. A nightmare of paranoia, schizophrenia, necrophilism, and vampirism supervenes, in which the natural affections are perverted by the will to destroy. Poe's heroines—Berenice, Ligeia, Madeline, Morella, with the curious exception of the abstemious Eleanora—are ill-disguised vampires; his heroes become necromancers (in the root meaning of the word) whose wills, like the heroines' wills, defy the term of life to keep them equivocally "alive." This primary failure in human feeling results in the loss of the entire natural order of experience.

The second hypertrophy is the thrust of the will beyond the human scale of action. The evidence of this is on nearly every page of Poe's serious prose fiction. Poe's readers, es-

2. "Our Cousin, Mr. Poe," pp. 80–95 of this volume.

pecially the young, like the quotation from Glanvill that appears as the epigraph to "Ligeia": "Man does not yield himself to the angels, nor unto Death utterly, save only through the weakness of his feeble will." It is the theme of the major stories. The hero professes an impossibly high love of the heroine that circumvents the body and moves in upon her spiritual essence. All this sounds high and noble, until we begin to look at it more narrowly, when we perceive that the ordinary carnal relationship between man and woman, however sinful, would be preferable to the mutual destruction of soul to which Poe's characters are committed. The carnal act, in which none of them seems to be interested, would witness a commitment to the order of nature, without which the higher knowledge is not possible to man. The Poe hero tries in self-love to turn the soul of the heroine into something like a physical object which he can know in direct cognition and then possess.

Thus we get the third hypertrophy of a human faculty: the intellect moving in isolation from both love and the moral will, whereby it declares itself independent of the human situation in the quest of essential knowledge.

The three perversions necessarily act together, the action of one implying a deflection of the others. But the actual emphases that Poe gives the perversions are richer in philosophical implication than his psychoanalytic critics have been prepared to see. To these ingenious persons, Poe's works have almost no intrinsic meaning; taken together they make up a *dossier* for the analyst to peruse before Mr. Poe steps into his office for an analysis. It is important at this point to observe that Poe takes for granted the old facultative psychology of intellect, will and feeling. If we do not observe this scheme, and let it point our enquiry, we shall fail to understand two crucial elements in Poe: first, that Poe's symbols refer to a known tradition of thought, an intelligible order, apart from what he was as a man, and are not merely the index to a compulsive neurosis; and, secondly, that the symbols, cast into the framework of the three faculties, point towards this larger philosophical dimension, implicit in the serious stories, but very much at the surface in certain of Poe's works that have been almost completely ignored.

I shall discuss here these neglected works: *The Conversation of Eiros and Charmion, The Colloquy of Monos and Una, The Power of Words*, and *Eureka.* The three first are dialogues between spirits in heaven, after the destruction of the earth; all four set forth a cataclysmic end of the world, modelled on the Christian eschatology. We shall see that *Eureka* goes further, and offers us a semi-rational vision of the final disappearance of the material world into the first spiritual Unity, or God.

It would be folly to try to see in these works the action of a first-rate philosophical mind; there is ingenuity rather than complex thinking. What concerns us is the relation of the semi-philosophical works to Poe's imaginative fiction; that is, a particular relation of the speculative intellect to the work of imagination. I shall have to show that Poe, as a critical mind, had only a distant if impressive insight into the disintegration of the modern personality; and that this insight was not available to him as an imaginative writer, when he had to confront the human situation as a whole man. He was the victim of a disintegration that he seems only intermittently to have understood. Poe is thus a man we must return to: a figure of transition, who retains a traditional insight into a disorder that has since become typical, without being able himself to control it.

Before we examine this insight it will be necessary to fix more clearly in mind than I have yet done the character of

Poe as a transitional man. Madame Raïssa Maritain, in a valuable essay, *Magie, Poésie, et Mystique*,[3] says:

Je ne vois guère de place dans la cosmologie d'Edgar Poe pour des recherches de recettes magiques. Et moins encore dans sa poésie, qui a toujours été parfaitement libre de toute anxiété de ce genre, et dont il n'aurait jamais voulu faire un instrument de pouvoir.

[I see little place in the cosmology of Edgar Poe for the pursuit of magic recipes. And still less in his poetry, which was always perfectly free of all anxiety of this kind, and of which he never wished to make an instrument of power.]

I am not sure that Madame Maritain is entirely right about the absence of magic, but there is no doubt that Poe *as poet* accepted certain limitations of language. He accepted them in practice. The obscurity of Poe's poetic diction is rather vagueness than the obscurity of complexity; it reflects his uncertain grasp of the relation of language to feeling, and of feeling to nature. But it is never that idolatrous dissolution of language from the grammar of a possible world, which results from the belief that language itself can be reality, or by incantation can create a reality: a superstition that comes down in French from Lautréamont, Rimbaud, and Mallarmé to the Surrealists, and in English to Hart Crane, Wallace Stevens, and Dylan Thomas. (I do not wish it to be understood that I am in any sense "rejecting" these poets, least of all under the rubric "superstition." When men find themselves cut off from reality they will frequently resort to magic rites to recover it—a critical moment of history that has its own relation to reality, from which poetry of great power may emerge.)

Poe, then, accepted his genre *in practice*. If the disorganized, synaesthetic sensibility arrives in the long run at a

3. *Situation de la Poésie:* Jacques et Raïssa Maritain (Paris, 1938), p. 58.

corresponding disintegration of the forms of grammar and rhetoric, it must be admitted that Poe stopped short at the mere *doctrine* of synaesthesia. In *The Colloquy of Monos and Una,* the angel Monos describes his passage into the after-life: "The senses were unusually active, although eccentrically so—assuming each other's functions at random. The taste and the smell were inextricably confounded, and became one sentiment, abnormal and intense."[4] But this is not the experience of synaesthesia rendered to our consciousness; to put it as Poe puts it is merely to consider it as a possibility of experience. Eighty years later we find its actuality in the language of an American poet:

> How much I would have bartered! the black gorge
> And all the singular nestings in the hills
> Where beavers learn stitch and tooth.
> The pond I entered once and quickly fled—
> I remember now its singing willow rim.

Rimbaud's "derangement of the senses" is realized. Why did not Poe take the next step and realize it himself? The question is unanswerable, for every writer is who he is, and not somebody else. The discoverer of a new sensibility seldom pushes it as far as language will take it; it largely remains a premonition of something yet to come. Another phase of Poe's disproportion of language and feeling appears in the variations of his prose style, which range from the sobriety and formal elegance of much of his critical writing, to the bathos of stories like *Ligeia* and *Berenice.* When Poe is not involved directly in his own feeling he can be a master of the *ordonnance* of 18th Century prose; there are passages in *The Narrative of Arthur Gordon Pym* that have the lucidity and intensity of Swift. But when he approaches the full human situation the traditional rhetoric

4. *Cf.* Baudelaire's *Correspondances:* "Les parfums, les couleurs, et les sons se répondent."

fails him. It becomes in his hands a humorless, insensitive machine whose elaborate motions conceal what it pretends to convey; for without the superimposed order of rhetoric the disorder hidden beneath would explode to the surface, where he would not be able to manage it. Poe is the transitional figure in modern literature because he discovered our great subject, the disintegration of personality, but kept it in a language that had developed in a tradition of unity and order. Madame Maritain is right in saying that he does not *use* language as magic. But he considers its possibility, and he thinks of language as a potential source of quasi-divine power. He is at the parting of the ways; the two terms of his conflict are thus more prominent than they would appear to be in a writer, or in an age, fully committed to either extreme. "When all are bound for disorder," says Pascal, "none seems to go that way."

Of the three dialogues that I shall discuss here, the first, *The Conversation of Eiros and Charmion,* published in 1839, was the earliest written. It is Poe's first essay at a catastrophic version of the disappearance of the earth: a comet passes over the earth, extracting the nitrogen from the atmosphere and replacing it with oxygen, so that the accelerated oxidation ends in world-wide combustion. But in treating the most unpromising materials Poe means what he says, although the occasions of journalism may not allow him to say all that he means. He *means* the destruction of the world. It is not only a serious possibility, it is a moral and logical necessity of the condition to which man has perversely brought himself.

Man's destruction of his relation to nature is the subject of the next dialogue, *The Colloquy of Monos and Una* (1841). From the perversion of man's nature it follows by a kind of Manichean logic that external nature itself must

be destroyed: man's surrender to evil is projected symbolically into the world.

This dialogue, the sequel to *The Conversation of Eiros
and Charmion*, is a theological fantasy of the destruction
of the earth by fire. I call the vision "theological" because
the destruction is not, as it was in the preceding dialogue,
merely the result of an interstellar collision. Monos says,
"That man, as a race, should not become extinct, I saw that
he must be *'born again.'* " Rebirth into the after-life is the
mystery that Monos undertakes to explain to Una; but first
he makes this long digression:

One word first, my Una, in regard to man's general condition
at this epoch. You will remember that one or two of the wise
men among our forefathers . . . had ventured to doubt the
propriety of the term "improvement" as applied to the progress
of our civilization. [They uttered] principles which should have
taught our race to submit to the guidance of the natural laws,
rather than attempt their control. Occasionally the poetic intellect—that intellect which we now feel to have been the most
exalted of all—since those truths to us were of the most enduring importance and could only be reached by that *analogy*
which speaks in proof-tones to the imagination alone, and to the
unaided reason bears no weight—occasionally did this poetic
intellect proceed a step farther in the evolving of the vaguely
philosophic, and find in the mystic parable that tells of the tree
of knowledge . . . death-producing, a distinct intimation that
knowledge was not meet for man in the infant condition of his
soul. . . .

Yet these noble exceptions from the general misrule served
but to strengthen it by opposition. The great "movement"—that
was the cant term—went on: a diseased commotion, moral and
physical. Art—the Arts—rose supreme, and, once enthroned, cast
chains upon the intellect which had elevated them to power.
Even while he stalked a God in his own fancy, an infantine im-
becility came over him. As might be supposed from the origin

of his disorder, he grew infected with system, and with abstraction. He enwrapped himself in generalities. Among other odd ideas, that of universal equality gained ground; and in the face of analogy and of God—in spite of the laws of graduation so visibly pervading all things . . . —wild attempts at an omnipresent Democracy were made. Yet this evil sprang necessarily from the leading evil—knowledge. . . . Meanwhile huge smoking cities arose, innumerable. Green leaves shrank before the hot breath of furnaces . . . now it appears that we had worked out *our own destruction in the perversion of our taste* [italics mine] or rather in the blind neglect of its culture in the schools. For in truth it was at this crisis that taste alone—that faculty which, *holding a middle position between the pure intellect and the moral sense* [italics mine], could never safely have been disregarded—it was now that taste alone could have led us gently back to Beauty, to Nature, and to Life.

. . . it is not impossible that the sentiment of the natural, had time permitted it, would have regained its old ascendancy over the harsh mathematical reasoning of the schools. . . . This the mass of mankind saw not, or, living lustily although unhappily, affected not to see.

I have quoted the passage at great length in the hope that a certain number of persons at a certain place and time will have read it. Poe's critics (if he have any critics) have not read it. When they refer to it, it is to inform us that Poe was a reactionary Southerner who disliked democracy and industrialism. It would not be wholly to the purpose but it would be edifying to comment on the passage in detail, for it adumbrates a philosophy of impressive extent and depth. When we remember that it was written in the United States in the early 1840's, an era of the American experiment that tolerated very little dissent, we may well wonder whether it was the result of a flash of insight, or of conscious reliance upon a wider European tradition. (My guess is that Poe's idea of "mathematical reasoning" was derived in part from Pascal's *L'esprit de géométrie,* his "taste" from *L'esprit de finesse.* This is a scholarly question that cannot be investigated here.)

A clue to the connection between Poe's historical and metaphysical insight, on the one hand, and the mode of his literary imagination, on the other, may be found in Paul Valéry's essay, "The Position of Baudelaire," where he says:

. . . the basis of Poe's thoughts is associated with a certain personal metaphysical system. By this system, if it directs and dominates and suggests the [literary] theories . . . *by no means penetrates them* [italics mine].[5]

His metaphysics was not available to him as experience; it did not *penetrate* his imagination. If we will consider together the "harsh mathematical reasoning of the schools" and the theory of the corruption of taste, we shall get a further clue to the Christian philosophical tradition in which Poe consciously or intuitively found himself. Taste is the discipline of feeling according to the laws of the natural order, a discipline of submission to a permanent limitation of man; this discipline has been abrogated by the "mathematical reasoning" whose purpose is the control of nature. Here we have the Cartesian split—taste, feeling, respect for the depth of nature, resolved into a subjectivism which denies the sensible world; for nature has become geometrical, at a high level of abstraction, in which "clear and distinct ideas" only are workable. The sensibility is frustrated, since it is denied its perpetual refreshment in nature: the operative abstraction replaces the rich perspectives of the concrete object. Reason is thus detached from feeling, and likewise from the moral sense, the third and

5. Paul Valéry: *Variety: Second Series,* trans. from the French by William Aspenwall Bradley (New York, 1938), "The Position of Baudelaire," p. 90.

executive member of the psychological triad, moving through the will. Feeling in this scheme being isolated or —as Mr. Scott Buchanan might put it—"occulted," it is strictly speaking without content, and man has lost his access to material forms. We get the hypertrophy of the intellect and the hypertrophy of the will. When neither intellect nor will is bound to the human scale, their projection becomes god-like, and man becomes an angel, in M. Maritain's sense of the term:

Cartesian dualism breaks man up into two complete substances, joined to one another none knows how: on the one hand, the body which is only geometrical extension; on the other, the soul which is only thought—an angel inhabiting a machine and directing it by means of the pineal gland.

. . . for human intellection is living and fresh only when it is centered upon the vigilance of sense perception. The natural roots of our knowledge being cut, a general drying up in philosophy and culture resulted, a drought for which romantic tears were later to provide only an insufficient remedy. . . . Affectivity will have its revenge.[6]

One cannot fail to see here a resemblance, *up to a point*, between the insights of Poe and of Maritain; but at that point appears the profound difference between a catastrophic acceptance and a poised estimation, of the Cartesian dualism. *The Colloquy of Monos and Una* is in the end a romantic tear, and in Poe's tales of perverted nature "affectivity" takes its terrible revenge.

We may discern the precise point at which Poe betrays his surrender to what I shall call the angelic fallacy: it is the point at which his conception of the "poetic intellect" becomes contradictory and obscure. This intellect speaks

6. Jacques Maritain: *The Dream of Descartes* (New York, 1944), Chap. 4, "The Cartesian Heritage," pp. 179–180. My debt to Mr. Maritain is so great that I hardly know how to acknowledge it.

to us, he says, "by analogy," in "proof tones to the imagination alone." The trap is the adverb *alone,* which contradicts the idea of analogy. He may have meant analogy to the natural world, the higher truths emerging, as they do in Dante, from a rational structure of natural analogy; but he could not have meant all this. And I suppose nobody else in the 19th Century understood analogy as a mode of knowledge. If the poetic intellect speaks "by analogy" it addresses more than the "imagination alone"; it engages also reason and cognition; for if it alone is addressed there is perhaps a minimum of analogy; if the imagination can work alone, it does so in direct intuition. And in fact in none of the essays and reviews does Poe even consider the idea of analogy. Its single mysterious appearance, in anything like its full historical sense, is in *The Colloquy of Monos and Una.* (It reappears in *Eureka,* where it means simple exemplification or parallelism.) In the "Poetic Principle," the poetic intellect moves independently, with only "incidental" connections with Pure Intellect and the Moral Sense; it is thus committed exclusively to Taste raised to an autonomous faculty. "Imagination is, possibly in man," says Poe in a footnote to his famous review of Halleck and Drake, "a lesser degree of the creative power of God." This is not far from the "esemplastic power" of the Primary Imagination, a Teutonic angel inhabiting a Cartesian machine named Samuel Taylor Coleridge.

Poe's exaltation of the imagination in its Cartesian vacuum foreshadows a critical dilemma of which we have been acutely aware in our own time. His extravagant claims for poetry do not in any particular exceed, except perhaps in their "period" rhetoric, the claims made by two later generations of English critics represented by Arnold and Richards. "Religion," said Arnold, "is morality touched with emotion." But religion, he said elsewhere, has attached itself to the "fact," by which he meant science; so religion has failed us. Therefore "the future of poetry is immense" because it is its own fact; that is to say, poetry is on its own, whatever its own may be—perhaps its own emotion, which now "touches" poetry instead of religion. Therefore poetry will save us, although it has no connection with the Cartesian machine running outside my window, or inside my vascular system. (Mr. Richards' early views I have discussed on several occasions over many years; I am a little embarrassed to find myself adverting to them again.) In Richards' writings, particularly in a small volume entitled *Science and Poetry* (1926), he tells us that the pseudo-statements of poetry—poetry on its own—cannot stand against the "certified scientific statement" about the facts which for Arnold had already failed both religion and poetry. Nevertheless poetry will save us because it "orders our minds"—but with what? For Mr. Richards, twenty-five years ago, the Cartesian machine was doing business as usual. Poetry would have to save us by ordering our minds with something that was not true.

Poe's flash of unsustained insight, in *The Colloquy of Monos and Una*, has, I submit, a greater dignity, a deeper philosophical perspective, and a tougher intellectual fibre, than the academic exercises of either Arnold or Mr. Richards. (I still reserve the right to admire both of these men.) Poe is not so isolated as they, in a provincialism of *time*. He still has access, however roundabout, to the great framework of the Aristotelian psychology to which the literature of Europe had been committed for more than two thousand years: this was, and still is for modern critics, an empirical fact that must be confronted if we are to approach literature with anything better than callow systems of psychological analysis, invented overnight, that put the imaginative work of the past at a distance seriously greater than that of time.

Poe with perfect tact puts his finger upon the particular function, feeling, that has been blighted by the abstraction of the pure intellect into a transcendental order of its own. He will let neither pure intellect nor the pure moral will (both having been purified of "nature") dominate poetry; he sees that poetry must be centered in the disciplined sense-perception which he inadequately calls taste; and he thus quite rightly opposes the "heresy of the didactic" and the "mathematical reasoning of the schools." He opposes both, but he gives in to the latter. Poe's idolatry of reason, ranging from the cryptogram and the detective story to the panlogism of *Eureka,* is too notorious to need pointing out. The autonomy of the will is in part the theme of the greater stories; and the autonomy of poetry, rising contradictorily and mysteriously from the ruin of its source in feeling, reflects "a lesser degree of the creative power of God." It is the creative power of the Word, man's *spoken* word, an extravagant and slippery pun on the Logos.

I now come to the third dialogue, *The Power of Words,* published in 1845, a fable in which the angelic imagination[7] is pushed beyond the limits of the angelic intelligence to the point at which man considers the possibility of creative power through verbal magic. The angels in this dialogue not only know essence directly; they also have the power of physical creation by means of *words.* We may ask here why, if Poe's insight was as profound as I think it was, he succumbed to a force of disintegration that he understood? An answer to this question is difficult. Insights of the critical intelligence, however impressive, will not always

7. Strictly speaking, an *angelic imagination* is not possible. Angels by definition have unmediated knowledge of essences. See pp. 37–39.

correct, they may never wholly rise above, the subtle and elusive implications of the common language to which the writer is born. As Dante well understood, this is the primary fact of his culture that he has got to reckon with. The culture of the imaginative writer is, first of all, the elementary use of language that he must hear and learn in childhood, and, in the end, not much more than a conscious manipulation of what he had received from life before the age of seven. Poe understood the spiritual disunity that had resulted from the rise of the demi-religion of scientism, but by merely opposing its excesses with equally excessive claims for the "poetic intellect," he subtly perpetuated the disunity from another direction. He set up, if we may be allowed the figure, a parallelogram of forces colliding by chance from unpredicted directions, not proceeding from a central unity. Although he was capable of envisaging the unified action of the mind through the three faculties, his own mind acted upon its materials now as intellect, now as feeling, now as will; never as all three together. Had he not been bred in a society committed to the rationalism of Descartes and Locke by that eminent angel of the rationalistic Enlightenment, Thomas Jefferson?[8] Such commitments probably lie so deep in one's sensibility that mere intellectual conviction, Poe's "unaided reason," can scarcely reach them. Perhaps this discrepancy of belief and feeling exists in all ages, and creates the inner conflicts from which poetry comes. If this points to something in the nature of the literary imagination, we are bound to say that it will always lie a little beyond our understanding.

By the time Poe came to write his fable of the power of words, the angels of omnipotent reason could claim a vic-

8. In the Virginia of Poe's time the subjects of conversation and reading were almost exclusively politics and theology. The educated Virginian was a deist by conviction and an Anglican or a Presbyterian by habit.

tory. The scene is again the after-life; the characters two angels who meet in interstellar space after the destruction of the earth—a disaster assumed in all three of the dialogues and in *Eureka,* and a possible eventuality in most of Poe's tales. (One scarcely needs to be reminded of the collapse of the world of Roderick Usher.) The probable meaning of this omnivorous symbol I shall try to glance at presently. The climax of the angels' talk will reveal the long way that Poe had come from the philosophic insight of 1841 to the full angelic vision of 1845:

Oinos—But why, Agathos, do you weep—and why, Oh why do your wings droop as we hover over this fair star—which is the greenest and yet most terrible of all we have encountered in our flight. Its brilliant flowers look like a fairy dream—but its fierce volcanoes like the passions of a turbulent heart.

Agathos—They *are*—they *are!* This wild star it is now three centuries since, with clasped hands, and with streaming eyes, at the feet of my beloved—I spoke it—with a few passionate sentences—into birth. Its brilliant flowers *are* the dearest of all unfulfilled dreams, and its raging volcanoes *are* the passions of the most turbulent and unhallowed of hearts.

How had Agathos created this beautiful but unhallowed object? By the "physical power of words," he tells Oinos. Madame Maritain is the only critic I have read who has had the perception to take seriously this dialogue; her comment is of great interest:

Eh bien, ce texte se réfère-t-il vraiment à une conception magique de la poésie et de la parole? Je ne crois pas. Nous avons affaire ici, comme dans *Eureka,* à une philosophie et une cosmologie panthéistiques, où tout mouvement et toute action participent a l'efficicacité d'une action divine.

[Does the text then really refer to a magical conception of poetry and of the word? I do not think so. We have to do here, as in *Eureka*, with a pantheistic philosophy and cosmology, where every movement and every action participates in the efficiency of a divine action.]

There can be no doubt about Poe's pantheism here and in *Eureka*, but in both works we cannot fail to detect special variations in the direction of deism. Madame Maritain quotes Léon Bloy on the eternal consequences of every action of divine grace for the human spirit, an ancient Christian doctrine connected with the belief in the Community of Saints, for which Pascal invented the great natural analogy:

The slightest movement affects the whole of nature; a stone cast into the sea changes the whole face of it. So, in the realm of Grace, the smallest act affects the whole by its results. Therefore everything has its importance.

In every action we must consider, besides the act itself, our present, past, and future conditions, and others whom it touches, and must see the connections of it all. *And so we shall keep ourselves well in check.*[9]

It almost seems as if Poe had just read this passage and had gone at once to his desk to begin *The Power of Words;* as if he had deliberately ignored the moral responsibility, the *check* upon human power, enjoined in the last sentence, and had concentrated upon Pascal's physical analogy for divine grace: "The slightest *movement* affects the whole of nature." One more step, and the "slightest movement," a spoken *word*, will act creatively. A failure of moral responsibility towards the universe would not necessarily issue in an act of physical creation; nor would action undertaken in the state of sanctifying grace produce stars that are both beautiful and hallowed, unless, of course, the *word* is a "magic recipe," incantatory magic, which I be-

9. Pascal's *Pensées*, with an English translation, brief notes and Introduction by H. F. Stewart, D.D. (New York, 1950), Adversaria 16; p. 377.

lieve we undoubtedly get in *The Power of Words*. This is not the same presumption as our own timid, superstitious reverence for an order of poetic language which creates its own reality, but rather a grandiose angelic presumption on the part of man. As usual, Poe is at least partly aware of what he is doing; for Agathos explains:

This power of retrogradation [Pascal's "the smallest action affecting the whole by its results"] in its absolute fulness and perfection—this faculty of referring *all* epochs, *all* effects to *all* causes—is of course the prerogative of the Deity alone—but in every variety of degree, short of absolute perfection, is the power itself exercised by the whole host of the Angelic intelligences.

This "power," of course, is not at this stage magical; it represents angelic knowledge rather than power. But when Agathos created his green star he was not yet an angel; he was still man, but man with the creative power, just short of divine perfection, of the angelic intelligences. Wasn't his power on earth actually greater than that of the angels of Christian theology? For they are not primary creators; they are the powerful but uncreative executives of the divine will. Agathos' doctrine transcends the ideal of mere angelic knowledge: it is superangelism. Man is not only an angel, he is God in his aspect of creativity. I remark almost with regret, mingled with uneasiness, that Poe proves my argument, perhaps too well. (When criticism thinks that it has proved anything, it has become angelic itself.) But this is not all: Oinos tells Agathos that he "remembers many successful experiments in what some philosophers were weak enough to denominate animalculae." And Agathos bows to the mathematicians: "Now the mathematicians . . . saw that the results of any given impulse were absolutely endless . . . these men saw, at the same time, that this species of analysis itself had within itself a capacity for indefinite progress. . . ." Mathematicians were about to achieve the omniscience of the Son, and biologists the creative power of the Father.

Are we to conclude that in these fantasies Poe "appears to yield himself completely to the idea of the moment"? I believe that Mr. Eliot's observation is inaccurate. Poe is quite capable of faking his science, and of appearing to take seriously his own wildest inventions; but the invention is the creaking vehicle of something deeper. What he really takes seriously, and what he yields to in the end, is not an *idea* of the moment. He is progressively mastered by one great idea, deeper than any level of conscious belief and developing to the end of his life at an ever increasing rate, until at last he is engulfed by it. It is his own descent into the maelstrom.

He arrives at it, or reaches the bottom of it, in *Eureka*, which he wrote in 1848, the year before his death. I shall not go so far as to connect, symbolically or prophetically, his death and the vision of the pit at the end of *Eureka*. We may only observe that the complete vision, of which the early works represent an approximation, immediately precedes his death. The proposition of which *Eureka* is to provide the "proof," he states at the beginning:

In the original unity of the first thing lies the secondary cause of all things, with the germ of their inevitable annihilation.

This "nothingness" is a dialectical conversion, not of one symbol into its opposite by analogy, as we see it in Dante, or even in Donne, but of an abstraction into its antithesis. Thesis: the omniscient intellect of man (of Poe as man) achieves a more than angelic knowledge in comprehending the structure and purpose of the created universe. Antithesis: the final purpose of the created universe is the extinction in its own unity of the omniscient intellect of man. There is no Hegelian synthesis. After the original act of divine creation, God withdraws into his deistic aloofness, leaving the separate and local acts of creation to man. This is the sphere of secondary creations which man as angelic delegate of God is empowered to perform. Thus, says Poe at the end of *Eureka,* not only is every man his own God, every man *is* God: every man the non-spatial center into which the universe, by a reverse motion of the atoms, will contract, as into its annihilation. God destroys himself in the eventual recovery of his unity. Unity equals zero. If Poe must at last "yield himself unto Death utterly," there is a lurid sublimity in the spectacle of his taking God along with him into a grave which is not smaller than the universe.

The material universe is in a state of radical disequilibrium, every atom striving to disengage itself from material forms and to return to the original center; but this is not a center in space. It is the Pascalian center which is the everywhere and nowhere, occupied by nothing. Since matter is merely the dialectical movement of attraction and repulsion, it will have ceased to exist when it rejoins the everywhere and nowhere. Space being emptied of matter, there is not even space, for space is that which is occupied by something. We are beyond the topless and bottomless abyss of Pascal.

The image of the abyss is in all of Poe's serious writings: the mirror in "William Wilson"; burial alive; the "tarn" into which the House of Usher plunges; the great white figure towards which Pym is being borne by a current of the sea; the pit over which the pendulum swings; the dead body containing the living soul of M. Valdemar; being walled up alive; the vertigo of the maelstrom.

Poe's most useful biographer, Professor Quinn, exhibits testimonials from modern physicists to bolster up with scientific authority a work in which he probably has little confidence. Let us assume, what may well be false, that *Eureka* from the scientific point of view of any age is nonsense. That would not make *Eureka* nonsense. "The glory of man," says Valéry in his essay on *Eureka*, "and something more than his glory, is to waste his powers on the void. . . . Thus it would seem that the history of thought can be summarized in these words: *It is absurd by what it seeks; great by what it finds.*" What did Poe's "absurd" essay in eschatology inadvertently find, if indeed it found anything but nothing? Valéry again (and again the French instruct us in Poe) points, in another context, to the central meaning of *Eureka*, without perhaps quite knowing that he has done so (for Paul Valéry was himself an archangel); he says: "As soon as we leave the bounds of the moment, as soon as we attempt to enlarge and extend our presence outside of itself, our forces are exhausted in our liberty." Is this always and under all conditions necessarily true? I think not; but it was particularly true of Poe.

It was true of him because in *Eureka* he circumvented the natural world and tried to put himself not in the presence of God, but in the seat of God. *The exhaustion of force as a consequence of his intellectual liberation from the sensible world*—that is my reading of Valéry as a gloss upon the angelism of Poe. The intellectual force is exhausted because in the end it has no real object. The human intellect cannot reach God as essence; only God as analogy. Analogy to what? Plainly analogy to the natural world; for there is nothing in the intellect that has not previously reached it through the senses. Had Dante arrived at the vision of God by way of sense? We must answer yes, because Dante's Triune Circle is light, which the finite intelligence can see only in what has already been seen by means of it. But Poe's center is that place—to use Dante's

great figure—"where the sun is silent." Since he refuses to
see nature, he is doomed to see nothing. He has overleaped
and cheated the condition of man. The reach of our imaginative enlargement is perhaps no longer than the ladder
of analogy, at the top of which we may see all, if we still
wish to *see* anything, that we have brought up with us from
the bottom, where lies the sensible world. If we take
nothing with us to the top but our emptied, angelic in-
tellects, we shall see nothing when we get there. Poe as
God sits silent in darkness. Here the movement of tragedy
is reversed: there is no action. Man as angel becomes a
demon who cannot initiate the first motion of love, and
we can feel only compassion with his suffering, for it is
potentially ours.

I have not supposed it necessary to describe in detail the
structure of *Eureka,* or to call attention to its great passages
of expository prose, which seem to me unsurpassed in their
kind in the 19th Century. I have not discussed Poe from
what is commonly known as the literary point of view. I
have tried to expound one idea, the angelism of the intellect, as one aspect of one writer. I do not hesitate in conclusion to commit Poe's heresy of the didactic, and to point a
moral. We shall be so exhausted in our liberty that we shall
have to take our final rest, not in the cool of the evening,
but in the dark, if any one of our modes decides to set up
in business for itself.

5

Our Cousin, Mr. Poe[1]

WHEN I WAS about fourteen there were in our house, along with the novels of John Esten Cooke, E. P. Roe, and Augusta Evans, three small volumes of Edgar Allan Poe. That, by my reckoning, was a long time ago. Even then the books were old and worn, whether from use (I suppose not) or from neglect, it did not occur to me to enquire. I remember, or imagine I remember the binding, which was blue, and the size, which was small, and the paper, which was yellow and very thin. One volume contained the Poems, prefaced by Lowell's famous "biography." In this volume I am sure, for I read it more than the others, was the well-known, desperate, and asymmetrical photograph, which I gazed at by the hour and which I hoped that I should some day resemble. Another volume contained most, or at least the most famous of the Tales: "Ligeia," which I liked best (I learned in due time that Poe had, too); "Morella" and "William Wilson," which I now like best; and "The Fall of the House of Usher," which was a little spoiled for me even at fourteen by the interjection of the "Mad Tryst of Sir Launcelot Canning."

1. Address delivered before the Poe Society of Baltimore on the centenary of his death, October 7, 1949; and repeated as a Bergen Lecture at Yale University, November 14, 1949.

Perhaps it was in this volume that I admired "Marginalia," the first "criticism" I remember reading; but I did not discern either the bogus erudition or the sense of high literature which Poe was the first American to distinguish from entertainment and self-improvement through books; the merits as well as the defects went over my head. "Marginalia" could not at any rate have been in the third volume, which was given to a single long work: *Eureka—A Prose Poem*. This astrophilosophical discourse, which the late Paul Valéry took more seriously than any English or American critic ever did, fell in with my readings in popular astronomical books. In the backyard I arranged in a straight line peas, cherries, and oranges, in the proportionate sizes and distances of the sun and planets, and some hundreds of feet away (an inch perhaps to a thousand light-years) an old volley ball of my elder brothers' to represent Alpha Lyrae.

Later, on another occasion, I expect to examine *Eureka* at length, as I read it now, not as I read it at fourteen; yet before I leave it I must mention two other circumstances of my boyhood reading and the feeling that accompanied it. It lives for me as no later experience of ideas lives, because it was the first I had. The "proposition" that Poe undertook to demonstrate has come back to me at intervals in the past thirty-six years with such unpredictable force that now I face it with mingled resignation and dismay. I can write it without looking it up:

In the original unity of the first thing lies the secondary cause of all things, with the germ of their inevitable annihilation.

This is not the place to try to say what Poe meant by it. I could not, at fourteen, have guessed what it meant even after I had read the book; yet it is a fact of my boyhood (which I cannot suppose unique) that this grandiose for-

mula for cosmic cataclysm became a part of my consciousness through no effort of my own but seemed to come to
me like a dream, and came back later, like a nursery
rhyme, or a tag from a popular song, unbidden.

The other circumstance I am surer of because it was a
visible fact, a signature in faded brown ink on the fly-leaf
of *Eureka:* it told me years later that the three volumes
had been printed earlier than 1870, the year the man who
had owned them died. He was my great-grandfather. My
mother had said, often enough, or on some occasion that
fixed it in memory, that her grandfather had "known Mr.
Poe." (She was of the era when all eminent men, living or
recently dead, were "Mr.") I knew as a boy that my great-
grandfather had been a "poet," and in 1930 I found some
of his poems, which I forbear to discuss. He had for a
while been editor of the *Alexandria Gazette* at about the
time of Mr. Poe's death. Both were "Virginians," though
Virginians of somewhat different schools and points of
view. I can see my great-grandfather in Poe's description
of a preacher who called upon him in the summer of 1848:
"He stood smiling and bowing at the madman Poe."

I have brought together these scattered memories of my
first reading of a serious writer because in discussing any
writer, or in coming to terms with him, we must avoid the
trap of mere abstract evaluation, and try to reproduce the
actual conditions of our relation to him. It would be difficult for me to take Poe up, "study" him, and proceed to a
critical judgment. One may give these affairs the look of
method, and thus deceive almost everybody but oneself.
In reading Poe we are not brought up against a large, artic-
ulate scheme of experience, such as we see adumbrated in
Hawthorne or Melville, which we may partly sever from
personal association, both in the writer and in ourselves.
Poe surrounds us with Eliot's "wilderness of mirrors," in

which we see a subliminal self endlessly repeated or, turning, a new posture of the same figure. It is not too harsh, I think, to say that it is stupid to suppose that by "evaluating" this forlorn demon in the glass, we dispose of him. For Americans, perhaps for most modern men, he is with us like a dejected cousin: we may "place" him but we may not exclude him from our board. This is the recognition of a relationship, almost of the blood, which we must in honor acknowledge: what destroyed him is potentially destructive of us. Not only this; we must acknowledge another obligation, if, like most men of my generation, we were brought up in houses where the works of Poe took their easy place on the shelf with the family Shakespeare and the early novels of Ellen Glasgow. This is the obligation of loyalty to one's experience: he was in our lives and we cannot pretend that he was not. Not even Poe's great power in Europe is quite so indicative of his peculiar "place" as his unquestioned, if unexamined, acceptance among ordinary gentle people whose literary culture was not highly developed. The horrors of Poe created not a tremor in the bosoms of young ladies or a moment's anxiety in the eyes of vigilant mothers. I suppose the gentlemen of the South did not read him much after his time; in his time, they could scarcely have got the full sweep and depth of the horror. Nothing that Mr. Poe wrote, it was said soon after his death, could bring a blush to the cheek of the purest maiden.

But I doubt that maidens read very far in the Tales. If they had they would have found nothing to disconcert the image that Miss Susan Ingram recorded from a visit of Poe to her family a few weeks before his death:

Although I was only a slip of a girl and he what seemed to me then quite an old man, and a great literary one at that, we got on together beautifully. He was one of the most courteous gentlemen I have ever seen, and that gave great charm to his manner. None of his pictures that I have ever seen look like the picture of Poe that I keep in my memory . . . there was something in his face that is in none of them. Perhaps it was in the eyes.

If he was a madman he was also a gentleman. Whether or not we accept Mr. Krutch's theory,[2] we know, as this sensible young lady knew, that she was quite safe with him. A gentleman? Well, his manners were exemplary (when he was not drinking) and to the casual eye at any rate his exalted idealization of Woman (even of some very foolish women) was only a little more humorless, because more intense, than the standard cult of Female Purity in the Old South.

What Mr. Poe on his own had done with the cult it was not possible then to know. A gentleman and a Southerner, he was not quite, perhaps, a Southern gentleman. The lofty intellect of Ligeia, of Madeline, of Berenice, or of Eleanora, had little utility in the social and economic structure of Virginia, which had to be perpetuated through the issue of the female body, while the intellect, which was public and political, remained under the supervision of the gentlemen. Although Morella had a child (Poe's only heroine, I believe, to be so compromised), she was scarcely better equipped than Virginia Clemm herself to sustain more than the immaculate half of the vocation of the Southern lady. "But the fires," writes Morella's narrator-husband, "were not of Eros." And we know, at the end of the story, that the daughter is no real daughter but, as Morella's empty "tomb" reveals, Morella herself come back as a vampire to wreak upon her "lover" the vengeance due him. Why is it due him? Because, quite plainly, the lover lacked, as he always lacked with his other heroines,

2. The theory that Poe was sexually impotent.

the "fires of Eros." The soul of Morella's husband "burns with fires it had never before known . . . and bitter and tormenting to my spirit was the gradual conviction that I could in no manner define their unusual meaning, or regulate their vague intensity." Perhaps in the soul of John Randolph alone of Virginia gentlemen strange fires burned. The fires that were not of Eros were generally for the land and oratory, and the two fires were predictably regulated.

Poe's strange fire is his leading visual symbol, but there is not space in an essay to list all its appearances. You will see it in the eye of the Raven; in "an eye large, liquid, and luminous beyond comparison," of Roderick Usher; in the burning eye of the old man in "The Tell-Tale Heart"; in "Those eyes! those large, those shining, those divine orbs," of the Lady Ligeia. Poe's heroes and heroines are always burning with a hard, gem-like flame—a bodyless exaltation of spirit that Poe himself seems to have carried into the drawing-room, where its limited visibility was sufficient guarantee of gentlemanly behavior. But privately, and thus, for him, publicly, in his stories, he could not "regulate its vague intensity."

I cannot go into this mystery here as fully as I should like; yet I may, I think, ask a question: Why did not Poe use explicitly the universal legend of the vampire? Perhaps some instinct for aesthetic distance made him recoil from it; perhaps the literal, business-like way the vampire went about making its living revolted the "ideality" of Poe. At any rate D. H. Lawrence was no doubt right in describing as vampires his women characters; the men, soon to join them as "undead," have by some defect of the moral will, made them so.

The mysterious exaltation of spirit which is invariably the unique distinction of his heroes and heroines is not quite, as I have represented it, bodyless. *It inhabits a human body but that body is dead. The spirits prey upon one another with destructive fire which is at once pure of lust and infernal.* All Poe's characters represent one degree or another in a movement towards an archetypal condition: the survival of the soul in a dead body; but only in "The Facts in the Case of Monsieur Valdemar" is the obsessive subject explicit.

In none of the nineteenth-century comment on "The Fall of the House of Usher" that I have read, and in none of our own period, is there a feeling of shock, or even of surprise, that Roderick Usher is in love with his sister: the relation not being physical, it is "pure." R. H. Stoddard, the least sympathetic of the serious early biographers, disliked Poe's morbidity, but admitted his purity. The American case against Poe, until the first World War, rested upon his moral indifference, or his limited moral range. The range is limited, but there is no indifference; there is rather a compulsive, even a profound, interest in a moral problem of universal concern. His contemporaries could see in the love stories neither the incestuous theme nor what it meant, because it was not represented literally. The theme and its meaning as I see them are unmistakable: the symbolic compulsion that drives through, and beyond, physical incest moves towards the extinction of the beloved's will in complete possession, not of her body, but of her being; there is the reciprocal force, returning upon the lover, of self-destruction. Lawrence shrewdly perceived the significance of Poe's obsession with incestuous love. Two persons of the least dissimilarity offer the least physical resistance to mutual participation in the *fire* of a common being. Poe's most casual reader perceives that his lovers never do anything but contemplate each other, or pore upon the rigmarole of preposterously erudite, ancient books, most of which never existed. They are living in each other's insides, in the hollows of which burns the fire of will and intellect.

The fire is a double symbol; it lights and it burns. It is overtly the "light" of reason but as action it becomes the consuming fire of the abstract intellect, without moral significance, which invades the being of the beloved. It is the fire that, having illuminated, next destroys. Lawrence is again right in singling out for the burden of his insight the epigraph to "Ligeia," which Poe had quoted from Glanvill: "Man does not yield himself to the angels, nor unto death utterly, save through the weakness of his own feeble will." Why do these women of monstrous will and intellect turn into vampires? Because, according to Lawrence, the lovers have not subdued them through the body to the biological level, at which sanity alone is possible, and they retaliate by devouring their men. This view is perhaps only partly right. I suspect that the destruction works both ways, that the typical situation in Poe is more complex than Lawrence's version of it.

If we glance at "The Fall of the House of Usher" we shall be struck by a singular feature of the catastrophe. Bear in mind that Roderick and Madeline are brother and sister, and that the standard hyperaesthesia of the Poe hero acquires in Roderick a sharper reality than in any of the others, except perhaps William Wilson. His naked sensitivity to sound and light is not " regulated" to the forms of the human situation; it is a mechanism operating apart from the moral consciousness. We have here something like a capacity for mere sensation, as distinguished from sensibility, which in Usher is atrophied. In terms of the small distinction that I am offering here, sensibility keeps us in the world; sensation locks us into the self, feeding upon the disintegration of its objects and absorbing them into the void of the ego. The lover, circumventing the body into the secret being of the beloved, tries to convert the spiritual object into an object of sensation: the intellect which knows and the will which possesses are unnaturally turned upon that centre of the beloved which should remain inviolate.

As the story of Usher opens, the Lady Madeline is suffering from a strange illness. She dies. Her brother has, of course, possessed her inner being, and killed her; or thinks he has, or at any rate wishes to think that she is dead. This is all a little vague: perhaps he has deliberately entombed her alive, so that she will die by suffocation—a symbolic action for extinction of being. Why has he committed this monstrous crime? Sister though she is, she is nevertheless not entirely identical with him: she has her own otherness, of however slight degree, resisting his hypertrophied will. He puts her alive, though "cataleptic," into the "tomb." (Poe never uses graves, only tombs, except in "Premature Burial." His corpses, being half dead, are thus only half buried; they rise and walk again.) After some days Madeline breaks out of the tomb and confronts her brother in her bloody cerements. This is the way Poe presents the scene:

". . . Is she not hurrying to upbraid me for my haste? Have I not heard her footsteps on the stair? Do I not distinguish the heavy and horrible beating of her heart? Madman!"—here he sprang furiously to his feet, and shrieked out his syllables, as if in his effort he were giving up his soul—*Madman! I tell you that she now stands without the door!*"

As if in the superhuman energy of his utterance there had been found the potency of a spell, the huge antique panels to which the speaker pointed threw slowly back, upon the instant, their ponderous and ebony jaws. It was the work of the rushing gust—but then without those doors there *did* stand the lofty and enshrouded figure of the Lady Madeline of Usher. There was blood upon her white robes, and the evidence of some bitter struggle upon every portion of her emaciated frame. For a moment she remained trembling to and fro upon the threshold —then, with a low moaning cry, fell heavily inward upon the person of her brother, and in her violent and now final death-agonies, bore him to the floor a corpse, and a victim to the terrors he had anticipated.

Madeline, back from the tomb, neither dead nor alive, is in the middle state of the unquiet spirit of the vampire, whose heart-beats are "heavy and horrible." There is no evidence that Poe knew any anthropology; yet in some legends of vampirism the undead has a sluggish pulse, or none at all. In falling prone upon her brother she takes the position of the vampire suffocating its victim in a sexual embrace. By these observations I do not suggest that Poe was conscious of what he was doing; had he been, he might have done it even worse. I am not saying, in other words, that Poe is offering us, in the Lady Madeline, a vampire according to Bram Stoker's specifications. An imagination of any power at all will often project its deepest assumptions about life in symbols that duplicate, without the artist's knowledge, certain meanings, the origins of which are sometimes as old as the race. If a writer ambiguously exalts the "spirit" over the "body," and the spirit must live wholly upon another spirit, some version of the vampire legend is likely to issue as the symbolic situation.

Although the action is reported by a narrator, the fictional point of view is that of Usher: it is all seen through his eyes. But has Madeline herself not also been moving towards the cataclysmic end in the enveloping action outside the frame of the story? Has not her *will to know* done its reciprocal work upon the inner being of her brother? Their very birth had violated their unity of being. They must achieve spiritual identity in mutual destruction. The physical symbolism of the fissured house, of the miasmic air, and of the special order of nature surrounding the House of Usher and conforming to the laws of the spirits inhabiting it—all this supports the central dramatic situation, which moves towards spiritual unity through disintegration.

In the original unity of the first thing lies the secondary cause of all things, with the germ of their inevitable annihilation.

Repeated here, in the context of the recurrent subject of the Tales, the thesis of *Eureka* has a sufficient meaning and acquires something of the dignity that Valéry attributed to it. Professor Quinn adduces quotations from mathematical physicists to prove that Poe, in *Eureka*, was a prophet of science. It is a subject on which I am not entitled to an opinion. But even if Professor Quinn is right, the claim is irrelevant, and is only another version of the attempt today to make religion and the arts respectable by showing that they are semi-scientific. Another sort of conjecture seems to me more profitable: that in the history of the moral imagination in the nineteenth century Poe occupies a special place. No other writer in England or the United States, or, so far as I know, in France, went so far as Poe in his vision of dehumanized man.

His characters are, in the words of William Wilson's double, "dead to the world"; they are machines of sensation and will, with correspondences, in the physical universe, to particles and energy. Poe's engrossing obsession in *Eureka* with the cosmic destiny of man issued in a quasi-cosmology, a more suitable extension of his vision than any mythology, home-made or traditional, could have offered him. The great mythologies are populous worlds, but a cosmology need have nobody in it. In Poe's, the hyperaesthetic egoist has put all other men into his void: he is alone in the world, and thus dead to it. If we place Poe against the complete Christian imagination of Dante, whom he resembles in his insistence upon a cosmic extension of the moral predicament, the limits of his range are apparent, and the extent of his insight within those limits. The quality of Poe's imagination can be located, as I see it, in only two places in Dante's entire scheme of the after-life: Cantos XIII and XXXII of the *Inferno*. In Canto XIII, the Harpies feed upon the living trees enclosing the shades of suicides—those "violent against themselves," who will not resume their bodies at the Resurrection, for "man may not have what he takes from himself." In XXXII, we are in Caïna, the ninth circle, where traitors to their kin lie half buried in ice, up to the pubic shadow—"where the doleful shades were . . . sounding with their teeth like storks." Unmotivated treachery, for the mere intent of injury, and self-violence are Poe's obsessive subjects. He has neither Purgatory nor Heaven; and only two stations in Hell.

Let us turn briefly to the question of Poe's style. He has several styles, and it is not possible to damn them all at once. The critical style, which I shall not be able to examine here, is on occasion the best; he is a lucid and dispassionate expositor, he is capable of clear and rigorous logic (even from mistaken premises, as in "The Rationale of Verse"), when he is not warped by envy or the desire to flatter. He is most judicial with his peers, least with his inferiors, whom he either overestimates or wipes out. As for the fictional style, it, too, varies; it is perhaps at its sustained best, in point of sobriety and restraint, in the tales of deduction. Exceptions to this observation are "Descent into the Maelström", "The Narrative of Arthur Gordon Pym," and perhaps one or two others in a genre which stems from the eighteenth-century "voyage." These fictions demanded a Defoe-like verisimilitude which was apparently beyond his reach when he dealt with his obsessive theme. Again I must make an exception: "William Wilson," one of the serious stories (by serious, I mean an ample treatment of the obsession), is perspicuous in diction and on the whole credible in realistic detail. I quote a paragraph:

The extensive enclosure was irregular in form, having many capacious recesses. Of these, three or four of the largest constituted the play-ground. It was level, and covered with a hard fine gravel. I well remember it had no trees, nor benches, nor anything similar within it. Of course it was in the rear of the house. In front lay a small parterre, planted with box and other shrubs, but through this sacred division we passed only upon rare occasions indeed—such as a first advent to school or a final departure hence, or perhaps, when a parent or a friend having called upon us, we joyfully took our way home for the Christmas or midsummer holidays.

It is scarcely great prose, but it has an eighteenth-century directness, and even elegance, of which Poe was seldom capable in his stories. I surmise that the playground at Dr. Bransby's school at Stoke-Newington, where, as a child, he was enrolled for five years, recalled one of the few periods of his life which he could detach from the disasters of manhood and face with equanimity. Now a part of the description of the Lady Ligeia:

. . . I examined the contour of the lofty and pale forehead—it was faultless—how cold indeed that word when applied to a majesty so divine!—the skin rivalling the purest ivory, the commanding extent and repose, the gentle prominence of the regions above the temples; and the raven-black, the glossy, the luxuriant, the naturally curling tresses, setting forth the full force of the Homeric epithet, "hyacinthine." I looked at the delicate outline of the nose. . . .

But I refrain. It is easy enough to agree with Aldous Huxley and Yvor Winters, and dismiss this sort of ungrammatical rubbish as too vulgar, or even too idiotic, to reward the time it takes to point it out. But if Poe is worth understanding at all (I assume that he is), we might begin by asking why the writer of the lucid if not very distinguished passage from "William Wilson" repeatedly fell into the bathos of "Ligeia." I confess that Poe's serious style at its typical worst makes the reading of more than one story at a sitting an almost insuperable task. The Gothic glooms, the Venetian interiors, the ancient wine-cellars (from which nobody ever enjoys a vintage but always drinks "deep")—all this, done up in a glutinous prose, so fatigues one's attention that with the best will in the world one gives up, unless one gets a clue to the power underlying the flummery.

I have tried in the course of these remarks to point in the direction in which the clue, as I see it, is to be found. I do not see it in the influence of the Gothic novel. This was no doubt there; but no man is going to use so much neo-Gothic, over and over again, unless he means business with it; I think that Poe meant business. If the Gothic influence had not been to hand, he would have invented it, or something equally "unreal" to serve his purpose. His purpose in laying on the thick décor was to simulate sensation. Poe's sensibility, for reasons that I cannot surmise here, was almost completely improverished. He could feel little but the pressure of his predicament, and his perceptual powers remained undeveloped. Very rarely he gives us a real perception because he is not interested in anything that is alive. Everything in Poe is dead: the houses, the rooms, the furniture, to say nothing of nature and of human beings. He is like a child—all appetite without sensibility; but to be in manhood all appetite, all will, without sensibility, is to be a monster: to feed spiritually upon men without sharing with them a real world is spiritual vampirism. The description of Ligeia's head is that of a dead woman's.

Does it explain anything to say that this is necrophilism? I think not. Poe's prose style, as well as certain qualities of his verse,[3] expresses the kind of "reality" to which he had access: I believe I have indicated that it is a reality sufficiently terrible. In spite of an early classical education and a Christian upbringing, he wrote as if the experience of these traditions had been lost: he was well ahead of his time. He could not relate his special reality to a wider context of insights—a discipline that might have disciplined his prose. From the literary point of view he combined the primitive and the decadent: primitive, because he had neither history nor the historical sense; decadent, because he was the conscious artist of an intensity which lacked moral perspective.

But writers tend to be what they are; I know of no way to make one kind into another. It may have been a con-

3. I expect to examine Poe's verse on another occasion. It may be remarked that his verse rhythms are for the metronome, not the human ear. Its real defects are so great that it is not necessary to invent others, as Mr. T. S. Eliot seems to do in *From Poe to Valéry* (New York, 1949). Thus Mr. Eliot (and I cite only one of his observations that seem to me wrong) complains that "the saintly days of yore" could not be an appropriate time for the Raven to have lived. Elijah was fed by Ravens, a bird which was almost extinct in America in the 1840's. Ravens frequently fed hermits and saints and were in fact a fairly standard feature of saintly equipment.

dition of Poe's genius that his ignorance should have been what it was. If we read him as formal critics we shall be ready to see that it was another condition of his genius that he should never produce a poem or a story without blemishes, or a critical essay that, despite its acuteness in detail, does not evince provincialism of judgment and lack of knowledge. We must bear in mind Mr. Eliot's remark that Poe must be viewed as a whole. Even the fiction and the literary journalism that seem without value add to his massive impact upon the reader.

What that impact is today upon other readers I cannot pretend to know. It has been my limited task to set forth here a little of what one reader finds in him, and to acknowledge in his works the presence of an incentive (again, for one man) to self-knowledge. I do not hesitate to say that had Poe not written *Eureka*, I should have been able, a man of this age, myself to formulate a proposition of "inevitable annihilation." I can only invite others to a similar confession. Back of the preceding remarks lies an ambitious assumption, about the period in which we live, which I shall not make explicit. It is enough to say that, if the trappings of Poe's nightmare strike us as tawdry, we had better look to our own. That particular vision in its purity (Poe was very pure) is perhaps not capable of anything better than Mr. Poe's ludicrous décor. Nor have persons eating one another up and calling it spiritual love often achieved a distinguished style either in doing it or in writing about it. It was not Ugolino, it was Dante who wrote about Ugolino with more knowledge than Ugolino had. Mr. Poe tells us in one of his simple poems that from boyhood he had "a demon in my view." Nobody then— my great-grandfather, my mother, three generations— believed him. It is time we did. I confess that his voice is so near that I recoil a little, lest he, Montressor, lead me into the cellar, address me as Fortunato, and wall me up alive. I should join his melancholy troupe of the undead, whose voices are surely as low and harsh as the grating teeth of storks. He is so close to me that I am sometimes tempted to enter the mists of pre-American genealogy to find out whether he may not actually be my cousin.

6

Is Literary Criticism
Possible?[1]

THE QUESTIONS that I propose to discuss in this essay
will fall into two main divisions. I shall undertake to
discuss, first, the teaching of literary criticism in the university. Since I am not able to *define* literary criticism I
shall be chiefly concerned with the idea of a formal relation; that is to say, supposing we knew what criticism is,
what relation would it have to the humanities, of which
it seems to be a constituent part? In the second division I
shall try to push the discussion a little further, towards a
question that has been acute in our time: Is literary criticism possible at all? The answer to this question ought
logically to precede the discussion of a formal relation,
for we ought to know what it is that we are trying to
relate to something else. But we shall never know this; we
shall only find that in teaching criticism we do not know
what we are teaching, even though criticism daily talks
about a vast material that we are in the habit of calling

1. Part I of this essay was read at a symposium on the humanities at
Vanderbilt University, October 20, 1950; Part II, at the Conference on the
Philosophical Bases of Literary Criticism at Harvard University, July 23,
1951. Both parts have been amplified.

the humanities. The mere fact of this witnesses our sense of a formal relation that ought to exist between two things of the nature of which we are ignorant.

I

Literary criticism as a member of the humanities I take to be a problem of academic statesmanship inviting what we hopefully call "solutions" of both the theoretical and the practical sort. Is literary criticism properly a branch of humanistic study? That is the theoretical question, to which I shall avoid the responsibility of giving the answer. Without this answer, we cannot hope to understand the practical question: What is the place of criticism in the humanities program; on what grounds should it be there (if it should be there at all), given the kind of education that the present teachers of the humanities bring to their work?

The two questions, the theoretical and the practical, together constitute the formal question; that is to say, whatever criticism and the humanities may be, we should have to discuss their relation in some such terms as I am suggesting. But before we follow this clue we must address ourselves more candidly to the fact of our almost total ignorance.

The three grand divisions of higher education in the United States are, I believe, the Natural Sciences, the Social Sciences, and the Humanities. Of the first, I am entirely too ignorant to speak. Of the social sciences I know little, and I am not entitled to suspect that they do not really exist; I believe this in the long run because I want to believe it, the actuality of a science of human societies being repellent to me, apart from its dubious scientific credentials. Of the humanities, the division with which as poet and critic I am presumably most concerned, one must speak with melancholy as well as in ignorance. For into the humanistic bag we throw everything that cannot qualify as a science, natural or social. This discrete mixture of hot and cold, moist and dry, creates in the bag a vortex, which emits a powerful wind of ineffectual heroics, somewhat as follows: We humanists bring within the scope of the humanities all the great records—sometimes we call them the remains: poetry, drama, pre-scientific history (Herodotus, Joinville, Bede)—of the experience of man *as* man; we are not concerned with him as vertebrate, biped, mathematician, or priest. Precisely, reply the social scientists; that is just what is wrong with you; you don't see that man is not man, that he is merely a *function;* and your records (or remains) are so full of error that we are glad to relegate them to professors of English, poets, and other dilettanti, those "former people" who live in the Past. The Past, which we can neither smell, see, taste, nor touch, was well labeled by our apostle, Mr. Carl Sandburg, as a bucket of ashes . . . No first-rate scientific mind is guilty of this vulgarity. Yet as academic statesmen, the humanists must also be practical politicians who know that they cannot stay in office unless they have an invigorating awareness of the power, and of the superior foot-work, of the third-rate mind.

As for literary criticism, we here encounter a stench and murk not unlike that of a battlefield three days after the fighting is over and the armies have departed. Yet in this war nobody has suggested that criticism is one of the social sciences, except a few Marxists, who tried fifteen years ago to make it a branch of sociology. History not long ago became a social science, and saved its life by losing it; and there is no reason why sociology "oriented" toward literature should not be likewise promoted, to the relief of everybody concerned. And whatever criticism may be, we should perhaps do well to keep it with the humanities, where it can profit by the sad example of Hilaire Belloc's Jim, who failed "To keep ahold of Nurse / For fear of getting something worse."

It may not be necessary to know what criticism is; it may be quite enough to see that it is now being written, that a great deal of it was written in the past, that it is concerned with one of the chief objects of humanistic study: literature. And we therefore study it either as an "area" in itself —that is, we offer courses in its history; or as a human interest in some past age—that is, we use criticism as one way of understanding the age of Johnson or the high Renaissance. Guided by the happy theory of spontaneous understanding resulting from the collision of pure intelligence with its object—a theory injected into American education by Charles W. Eliot—we expose the student mind to "areas" of humanistic material, in the confident belief that if it is exposed to enough "areas" it will learn something. If we expose it to enough "areas" in all three grand divisions, the spontaneous intelligence will automatically become educated without thought.

The natural sciences have a high-powered rationale of their daily conquests of nature. The social sciences have a slippery analogical[2] metaphor to sustain their self-confidence. The humanities modestly offer the vision of the historical lump. This lump is tossed at the student mind, which is conceived as the miraculous combination of the *tabula rasa* and innate powers of understanding. In short, the humanities have no rationale. We suppose that it is sufficient to show that a given work—a poem, a play, a critical "document"—came before or after some other poem, play, or critical "document," or was written when

2. Analogous to the natural sciences.

something else was happening, like Alexander's invasion of India or the defeat of the Armada. When these and other correlations are perceived, the result is understanding. But the result of correlation is merely the possibility of further correlation. Our modest capacity for true understanding is frustrated. For the true rationale of humanistic study is now what it has always been, even though now it is not only in decay, but dead. I allude to the arts of rhetoric.

By rhetoric I mean the study and the use of the figurative language of experience as the discipline by means of which men govern their relations with one another in the light of truth. Rhetoric presupposes the study of two prior disciplines, grammar and logic, neither of which is much pursued today, except by specialists.

These disciplines are no longer prerequisite even to the study of philosophy. An Eastern university offers a grandiose course in Greek philosophical ideas to sophomores who will never know a syllogism from a handsaw. A graduate student who, I was told, was very brilliant in nuclear physics, decided that he wanted to take a course in *The Divine Comedy*. (Why he wanted to study Dante I do not know, but his humility was impressive.) I was assured by the academic grapevine that he understood difficult mathematical formulae, but one day in class he revealed the fact that he could neither define nor recognize a past participle. At the end of the term he confessed that nobody had ever told him that the strategies of language, or the arts of rhetoric, could be as important and exacting a discipline as the theory of equations. He had thought courses in English a little sissified; he had not been told that it might be possible, after severe application, to learn how to read. He had learned to talk without effort in infancy, in a decadent democracy, and no doubt supposed that grammar came of conditioning, and that he would get it free.

Back of this homely exemplum stands a formidable specter whose name is Cultural Decay—at a time when men are more conscious of cultures than ever before, and stock their universities and museums with lumps of cultures, like inert geological specimens in a glass case. I am far from believing that a revival of the trivium, or the three primary liberal arts, would bring the dead bodies to life: revivals have a fatal incapacity to revive anything. But unless we can create and develop a hierarchy of studies that can lead not merely to further studies but to truth, one may doubt that the accelerating decline of modern culture will be checked.

Without quite knowing what literary criticism is, let us assume again that we are teaching it within the humanities division, usually in the English Department, either because it ought to be there or because nobody else wants it. For convenience we may think of the common relations between the work of the imagination and the teaching activity under four heads, which I shall put in the form of rhetorical questions:

(1) Can a given work, say *Clarissa Harlowe* or *Kublai Khan*, be "taught," in such a way as to make it understood, without criticism?

(2) Can the work be taught first, and the criticism then applied as a mode of understanding?

(3) Can the criticism be presented first and held in readiness for the act of understanding which could thus be simultaneous with the act of reading the novel or the poem?

(4) Is the purpose of teaching imaginative works to provide materials upon which the critical faculty may exercise itself in its drive toward the making of critical sys-

tems, which then perpetuate themselves without much reference to literature?

These four versions of the relation by no means exhaust its possible variations. The slippery ambiguity of the word criticism itself ought by now to be plain. But for the purposes of this localized discussion, which I am limiting for the moment to the question of how to teach, we may think of criticism as three familiar kinds of discourse about works of literature. (We must bear in mind not only our failure to know what criticism is, but another, more difficult failure resulting from it: the failure to know what literature is.) The three kinds of critical discourse are as follows: (1) acts of evaluation of literature (whatever these may be); (2) the communication of insights; and (3) the rhetorical study of the language of the imaginative work.

I am not assuming, I am merely pretending that any one of the three activities is to be found in its purity. To the extent that they may be separated, we must conclude that the two first, acts of evaluation and the communication of insights, cannot be taught, and that the third, rhetorical analysis, has not been taught effectively in this country since the rise of the historical method in literary studies.

When I first taught a college class, about eighteen years ago, I thought that anything was possible; but with every year since it has seemed a little more absurd to try to teach students to "evaluate" works of literature, and perhaps not less absurd to try to evaluate them oneself. The assumption that we are capable of just evaluation (a word that seems to have got into criticism by way of Adam Smith) is one of the subtler, if crude, abuses of democratic doctrine, as follows: all men ought to exercise independent judgment, and all men being equal, all are equally capable of it, even in literature and the arts. I have observed that

when my own opinions seem most original and independent they turn out to be almost wholly conventional.
An absolutely independent judgment (if such a thing were
possible) would be an absolutely ignorant judgment.

Shall the instructor, then, set before the class his own
"evaluations"? He will do so at the risk of disseminating a
hierarchy that he may not have intended to create, and
thus may be aborted, or at least stultified, the student's
own reading. It is inevitable that the instructor shall say
to the class that one poem is "better" than another. The
student, in the degree of his intelligence, will form clear
preferences or rejections that will do little harm if he
understands what they are. But the teaching of literature
through the assertion of preference will end up either as
mere impressionism, or as the more sinister variety of impressionism that Irving Babbitt detected in the absorption
of the literary work into its historical setting.

As to the communication of "insights," it would perhaps
be an inquiry without benefit to anybody to ask how this
elusive maid-of-all-work got into modern criticism. She is
here, and perhaps we ought to be grateful, because she is
obviously willing to do all the work. Insight could mean
two things, separately or taken together: the perception of
meanings ordinarily or hitherto undetected, and/or the
synthetic awareness that brings to the text similar or contrasting qualities from other works. These awarenesses are
the critical or receiving end of the Longinian "flash" proceeding from varying degrees of information and knowledge, unpredictable and largely unviable. They are doubtless a good thing for a teacher to have, but they cannot be
taught to others; they can be only exhibited. If insight is
like faith, a gift by the grace of God, there is no use in
teaching at all—if insight-teaching is our only way of
going about it. But if it is partly a gift and partly the result

of labor (as Longinus thought), perhaps the teacher could find a discipline of language to expound to the class, with the hope that a latent gift of insight may be liberated.

Rhetoric is an unpopular word today, and it deserves to be, if we understand it as the "pragmatic dimension" of discourse as this has been defined by Charles W. Morris, and other semanticists and positivists. In this view rhetoric is semantically irresponsible; its use is to move people to action which is at best morally neutral; or if it is good action, this result was no necessary part of the rhetorician's purpose. The doctrine is not new; it is only a pleasantly complex and double-talking revival of Greek sophistry. But if we think of rhetoric in another tradition, that of Aristotle and of later, Christian rhetoricians, we shall be able to see it as the study of the full language of experience, not the specialized languages of method.[3] Through this full language of experience Dante and Shakespeare could arrive at truth.

This responsible use implies the previous study of the two lower, but not inferior, disciplines that I have already mentioned. One of these was once quaintly known as "grammar," the art that seems to be best learned at the elementary stage in a paradigmatic language like Latin. I think of a homely exemplum that will illustrate one of the things that have happened since the decay of grammar. I had a student at the University of Chicago who wrote a paper on T. S. Eliot's religious symbolism, in which he

3. I hope it is plain by this time that by "rhetorical analysis" and the "study of rhetoric" I do not mean the prevailing *explication of texts*. If rhetoric is the *full* language of experience, its study must be informed by a peculiar talent, not wholly reducible to method, which I have in the past called the "historical imagination," a power that has little to do with the academic routine of "historical method." For a brilliant recent statement of this difference, see "Art and the Sixth Sense" by Philip Rahv, *Partisan Review*, March-April 1952, pp. 225–233. The "sixth sense" is the historical imagination.

failed to observe that certain sequences of words in "Ash Wednesday" are without verbs: he had no understanding of the relation of the particulars to the universals in Eliot's diction. The symbols floated, in this student's mind, in a void of abstraction; the language of the poem was beyond his reach. Is the domination of historical scholarship responsible for the decline of the grammatical arts? I think that it may be; but it would not follow from its rejection that these arts or their equivalent would rise again. (One must always be prepared for the rise of nothing.) My Chicago student was laudably trying to read the text of the poem; he had nothing but a good mind and good intentions to read it with. What he had done, of course, was to abstract Eliot's symbols out of their full rhetorical context, so that they had become neither Eliot's nor anybody else's symbols. They were thus either critically useless, or potentially useful in a *pragmatic dimension* of discourse where ideas may be *power*: as the fullback is said to "bull" through the opposing line. The rhetorical disciplines, which alone seem to yield something like the full import of the work of imagination, are by-passed; and we by-pass these fundamentals of understanding no less when we read our own language. All reading is translation, even in the native tongue; for translation may be described as the tact of mediation between universals and particulars in the complex of metaphor. As qualified translators we are inevitably rhetoricians. One scarcely sees how the student (like the Chicago student, who is also the Minnesota, the Harvard, and the Cornell student) can be expected to begin the study of rhetoric at the top, particularly if below it there is no bottom. If he begins at the top, as a "critic," he may become the victim of "insights" and "evaluations" that he has not earned, or he may parrot critical systems that his instructors have expounded or perhaps merely alluded to, in class. In any case, man being by nature, or by the nature of his language, a rhetorician, the student becomes a bad rhetorician. It is futile to expect him to be a critic when he has not yet learned how to read.

How can rhetoric, or the arts of language, be taught to-day? We are not likely to begin teaching something in which we do not believe: we do not believe in the uses of rhetoric because we do not believe that the full language of the human situation can be the vehicle of truth. We are not facing the problem when we circumvent it by asking the student to study the special languages of "criticism," in which we should like to believe. Can we believe in the language of humane truth without believing in the possibility of a higher unity of truth, which we must posit as *there*, even if it must remain beyond our powers of understanding? Without such a belief are we not committed to the assumption that literature has nothing to do with truth, that it is only illusion, froth on the historical current, the Platonic *gignomenon*? We languish, then, in the pragmatic vortex where ideas are disembodied into power; but power for what it is not necessary here to try to say. I turn now to literary criticism as it seems to be in itself, apart from any question of teaching it.

II

We have reached the stage of activity in individual criticism at which we begin to ask whether what we severally do has, or ought to have, a common end. What has a common end may be better reached, or at any rate more efficiently pursued, if the long ways to it are by-passed for the short ways—if happily we can agree on a common methodology, or at worst a few cooperating methodologies. The image that this enticing delusion brings to mind is that of the cheerful, patient bulldozer leveling off an uncharted landscape. The treeless plain thus made could be used as a desert—by those who can use deserts—or as an airfield from which to fly somewhere else.

The notes that follow I have put in the form of propositions, or theses, which either I or some imaginable person might be presumed to uphold at the present time. Some will be found to contradict others; but this is to be expected when we try to distinguish the aims and habits of literary critics over a period so long as a quarter of a century. The ten theses will affirm, deny, or question a belief or a practice.

I. Literary criticism is in at least one respect (perhaps more than one) like a mule: it cannot reproduce itself, though, like a mule, it is capable of trying. Its end is outside itself. If the great formal works of literature are not wholly autonomous, criticism, however theoretical it may become, is necessarily even less so. It cannot in the long run be practiced apart from what it confronts, that gives rise to it. It has no formal substance: it is always *about* something else. If it tries to be about itself, and sets up on its own, it initiates the infinite series: one criticism within another leading to another criticism progressively more formal-looking and abstract; or it is progressively more irrelevant to its external end as it attends to the periphery, the historical buzz in the rear of literature.

II. The more systematic and methodical, the "purer," criticism becomes, the less one is able to feel in it the presence of its immediate occasion. It tends more and more to *sound* like philosophical discourse. There are countless degrees, variations, and overlappings of method, but everyone knows that there are three typical directions that method may take: (1) Aesthetics, which aims at the ordering of criticism within a large synthesis of either experimental psychology or ontology; from the point of view of which it is difficult to say anything about literature that is not merely pretentious. For example: Goethe's Concrete Universal, Coleridge's Esemplastic Power, Croce's Expression. (2) Analysis of literary language, or "stylistics" (commonly supposed to be the orbit of the New Criticism). Without the correction of a total rhetoric, this *techné* must find its limit, if it is not at length to become only a habit, in the extreme "purity" of nominalism ("positivism") or of metaphysics. (3) Historical scholarship, the "purest" because the most methodical criticism of all, offers the historical reconstruction as the general possibility of literature, without accounting for the unique, miraculous superiority of *The Tempest* or of *Paradise Lost*.

III. When we find criticism appealing to phrases like "frame of reference," "intellectual discipline," or even "philosophical basis," it is not improper to suspect that the critic is asking us to accept his "criticism" on the authority of something in which he does not believe. The two first phrases contain perhaps hidden analogies to mathematics; the third, a metaphor of underpinning. This is nothing against them; all language is necessarily figurative. But used as I have indicated, the phrases have no ontological, or substantive, meaning. The critic is only avoiding the simple word truth, and begging the question. Suppose we acknowledge that the critic, as he begs this question, gives us at the same moment a new and just insight into a scene in *The Idiot* or *King Lear*. Yet the philosophical language in which he visibly expounds the insight may seem to reflect an authority that he has not visibly earned. The language of criticism had better not, then, try to be univocal. It is neither fish nor fowl, yet both, with that unpleasant taste that we get from fishing ducks.

IV. Literary criticism may become prescriptive and dogmatic when the critic achieves a coherence in the logical and rhetorical orders which exceeds the coherence of the imaginative work itself in those orders. We substitute with the critic a dialectical order for the elusive, and perhaps quite different, order of the imagination. We fall into the trap of the logicalization of parts discretely attended. This sleight of hand imposed upon the reader's good faith invites him to share the critic's own intellectual pride. Dazzled by the refractions of the critic's spectrum, the reader accepts as his own the critic's dubious superiority to the work as a whole. He is only attending serially to the separated parts in which he worships his own image. This is critical idolatry; the idols of its three great sects are the techniques of purity described in Thesis II.

V. If criticism undertakes the responsibility and the privilege of a strict theory of knowledge, the critic will need all the humility that human nature is capable of, almost the self-abnegation of the saint. Is the critic willing to test his epistemology against a selfless reading of *The Rape of the Lock, War and Peace,* or a lyric by Thomas Nashe? Or is his criticism merely the report of a quarrel between the imagined life of the work and his own "philosophy"? Has possession of the critic by a severe theory of knowledge interfered with the primary office of criticism? What is the primary office of criticism? Is it to expound and to elucidate, with as little distortion as possible, the knowledge of life contained by the novel or the poem or the play? What critic has ever done this?

VI. A work of the imagination differs from a work of the logical intellect in some radical sense that seems to lie beyond our comprehension. But this much may be said: the imaginative work admits of neither progressive correction nor substitution or rearrangement of parts; it is never obsolete, it is always up-to-date. Dryden does not "improve" Shakespeare; Shakespeare does not replace Dante, in the way that Einstein's physics seems to have "corrected" Newton's. There is no competition among poems. A good poem suggests the possibility of other poems equally good. But criticism is perpetually obsolescent and replaceable.

VII. The very terms of elucidation—the present ones, like any others—carry with them, concealed, an implicated judgment. The critic's rhetoric, laid out in his particular grammar, is the critic's mind. This enables him to see much that is there, a little that is there, nothing that is there, or something that is not there; but none of these with perfect consistency. We may ask again: to what extent is the critic obligated to dredge the bottom of his mind and to exhibit to an incredulous eye his own skeleton? We might answer the question rhetorically by saying: We are constantly trying to smoke out the critic's "position." This is criticism of criticism. Should we succeed in this game to our perfect satisfaction, we must be on guard lest our assent to or dissent from a critic's "position" mislead us into supposing that his gift of elucidation is correspondingly impressive or no good. If absolutely just elucidation were possible, it would also be philosophically sound, even though the critic might elsewhere announce his adherence to a philosophy that we should want to question.

VIII. If the implicated judgment is made overt, is there not in it an invitation to the reader to dismiss or to accept the work before he has read it? Even though he "read" the work first? (Part of this question is dealt with in Thesis V.) Is *a priori* judgment in the long run inevitable? What unformulated assumption lurks, as in the thicket, back of T. S. Eliot's unfavorable comparison of "Ripeness is all" with *"E la sua voluntade è nostra pace"*? Is Shakespeare's summation of life naturalistic, pagan, and immature? J. V.

Cunningham has shown that "Ripeness is all" is a statement within the natural law, quite as Christian as Dante's statement within the divine law. The beacon of conceptual thought as end rather than means in criticism is a standing menace to critical order because it is inevitable, human nature being what it is. One thing that human nature is, is "fallen."

IX. In certain past ages there was no distinct activity of the mind conscious of itself as literary criticism; for example, the age of Sophocles and the age of Dante. In the age of Dante the schoolmen held that poetry differed from scriptural revelation in its *historia,* or fable, at which, in poetry, the literal event could be part or even all fiction. But the other, higher meanings of poetry might well be true, in spite of the fictional plot, if the poet had the gift of anagogical, or spiritual, insight. Who was capable of knowing when the poet had achieved this insight? Is literary criticism possible without a criterion of absolute truth? Would a criterion of absolute truth make literary criticism as we know it unnecessary? Can it have a relevant criterion of truth without acknowledging an emergent order of truth in its great subject matter, literature itself?

X. Literary criticism, like the Kingdom of God on earth, is perpetually necessary and, in the very nature of its middle position between imagination and philosophy, perpetually impossible. Like man, literary criticism is nothing in itself; criticism, like man, embraces pure experience or exalts pure rationality at the price of abdication from its dual nature. It is of the nature of man and of criticism to occupy the intolerable position. Like man's, the intolerable position of criticism has its own glory. It is the only position that it is ever likely to have.

7

Johnson

on the

Metaphysical Poets

W HEN we feel disposed to dismiss Johnson's views on
the Metaphysical poets as prejudice, we ought to
consider whether we are not opposing one prejudice with
another, of another kind, between which sensible compromise is difficult or even impossible. I see no way to
refute Johnson's attack on the school of Donne short of
setting up an abstract critical dialectic which would have
little bearing upon how poetry is written in any age. I
should like to marshal here a set of prejudices, of my own,
as cogent as Johnson's, but that would be a feat beyond
my capacity, as it would surely be beyond the reach of
any critic less ignorant than myself. As a man of the first
half of the twentieth century, I have no doubt as many
prejudices as Johnson had, but I cannot be sure that I
understand mine as well as he understood his. The first
obstacle to our understanding of prejudice is the liberal
dogma that prejudice must not be entertained; it has, with
us, something of the private, the mantic, and the wilful. In
this positive ignorance we would do well to remember

with Mr. F. R. Leavis that Johnson lived in a "positive culture" which made it easier than it is today for a critic to undergo a "positive training" for his profession.[1] Johnson came to *The Lives of the Poets* when a great age of English poetry was about ending; he had lived through the age, he had formed his sensibility, and disciplined his mind, in it; and it was a poetry to which the Metaphysical style had contributed little. If we refuse to see him as a part of a positive culture, in which personal prejudice can at times, in certain persons, receive the discipline of objectivity which transcends the disorder of unacknowledged opinion, we shall the more readily see in our disagreements with him a failure of understanding on his part.

These general remarks will serve to expose the bias of the narrow enquiry that follows. Whether it is a proper field of enquiry cannot be determined in a short essay. I shall not be concerned with Johnson's criticism as a whole, or with the permanent value of his particular judgments; I shall try to investigate a contrast, very broadly conceived, in the use of figurative language, with Johnson on one side and the Metaphysical style on the other. For this purpose I quote, to begin with, four lines from Denham's "Cooper's Hill" and a part of Johnson's commentary:

1. I am indebted to Mr. Leavis for several observations ("Samuel Johnson," by F. R. Leavis, *The Importance of Scrutiny*, ed. Eric Bentley, pp. 57–75). W. B. C. Watkins' *Johnson on English Poetry Before 1660* is indispensable in any study of Johnson's views on Donne. I have not made much explicit use of W. K. Wimsatt's two excellent books, *The Prose Style of Samuel Johnson* (1941) and *Philosophic Words* (1948), but I could not have written this paper without them. T. S. Eliot's two unpublished lectures on Johnson, which I did not hear when he delivered them publicly in the United States in 1947, he kindly allowed me to read. I am not conscious of having "used," directly or by allusion, any of his ideas; but if I have, and particularly if I have got them wrong, I can only say that neither Mr. Eliot nor anybody else can be held responsible for what I may have done to him.

O could I flow like thee, and make thy stream
My great example, as it is my theme!
Though deep, yet clear; though gentle, yet not dull;
Strong without rage, without o'erflowing full.

The lines in themselves [says Johnson] are not perfect; for most
of the words, thus artfully opposed, are to be understood simply
on one side of the comparison, and metaphorically on the other;
and if there be any language which does not express intellectual
operations by material images, into that language they cannot
be translated.

Johnson adds that the passage has "beauty peculiar to itself, and must be numbered among those felicities which
cannot be produced at will by wit and labor. . . ." (If he
was right in saying that "almost every writer for a century
has imitated" the lines, we might reasonably expect him
to have turned upon them his best critical powers.) The
imperfection of the metaphor, he seems to say, lies in its
failure to work both ways; that is, the qualities that Denham would like to achieve in his style cannot be found
literally in the river. The literal and the metaphorical
cannot be reciprocally interchanged. I am a little puzzled
that Johnson should see in this discrepancy a defect; for
ordinarily it would be a defect from our point of view
today, but not from his: the approach to identity of
"vehicle" and "tenor" was not a feature of metaphor which
the neo-classical critics thought possible or desirable. Johnson I think has an altogether different point in mind.

If we look again at the third part of the sentence, we
shall be struck by the negatives in both the conditional and
the independent clause. What is Johnson getting at when
he says that it is the fault of the passage that the intellectual qualities which Denham desires cannot be "translated"
into non-material images? Remove the negatives and we
get something like this: If there is a language which can

express intellectual operations by material images, into that language the passage can be translated; but it cannot be translated into abstract language. And that is Johnson's real objection to the lines. The tenor of the figure, to be convincing, ought to have translatability into a high degree of abstraction; it ought to be detachable from the literal image of the flowing river. If we bring our own prejudices into play at this point, we should have to decide that Johnson's opinion of the lines is scarcely consistent with his calling them a "felicity" "which cannot be reproduced at will by wit and labor"; for, to parody Johnson himself, figurative language comes naturally if not elegantly to our lips; systematic abstraction is the result of labor. What Johnson seems to detect here is the doubtful application of the operations of the mind to the river; it is a one-way metaphor in which the tenor is compromised by the vehicle. I believe it is fair to say that Johnson liked his tenors straight, without any nonsense from the vehicles. His remark that the "particulars of resemblance are perspicaciously collected," seems incomprehensible.

Johnson would doubtless agree with us in finding little in common between Denham's lines and the fourth stanza of Donne's "A Nocturnall upon S. Lucie's Day." Let us look briefly at that stanza, as well as we can, with the eyes that Johnson turned upon Denham.

> But I am by her death, (which word wrongs her)
> Of the first nothing, the Elixer grown;
>> Were I a man, that I were one,
>> I needs must show; I should preferre,
>>> If I were any beast,
> Some ends, some means; Yea plants, yea stones detest,
> And love; All, all some properties invest;
> If I an ordinary nothing were,
> As shadow, a light, and body must be here.

I do not know how to paraphrase the tenor of these lines, because I run at once into Johnson's difficulties with Denham. There are probably no abstractions, more abstract than Donne's own language, into which the distinction between an "ordinary nothing" and the "Elixer" of the "first nothing" can be paraphrased. The tenor can be located only in its vehicle, the specific metaphorical structure of the passage. One of Johnson's counts against the Metaphysical poets was the failure to represent the "operations of intellect" (to say nothing of their wilful neglect of the "scenes of life" and the "prospects of nature"), a quality that Johnson found pre-eminently in Pope. Yet it must seem to us that Donne is more nearly an *intellectual* poet than Pope (if the designation have meaning at all), for many of Donne's poems are, at one level or another, semi-rational operations elaborately drawn out. (These misunderstandings seize upon one slippery term after another, which will never be fixed, though it is the perpetual task of criticism to misunderstand its "problems" in new terms at intervals of about fifty years.) Johnson knew Donne's poetry thoroughly, much of it by heart, and he quotes him extensively; but his scattered comment is so brief that we cannot reconstruct a coherent view. We can only surmise that he would have found it "improper" and "vicious" for a man to imagine himself less than an "ordinary nothing." He tells us that "whatever is improper or vicious is produced by a voluntary deviation from nature in pursuit of something new and strange."

No deviation from nature, in Johnson's sense, appears in Denham's lines, on the literal plane; but in being true to nature he is not able to use the river as an accurate vehicle for an "operation of intellect"; so he accepts the tenor "metaphorically" only; that is to say, he cannot really locate it, he finds it a little incredible. But in the stanza by

Donne is not the vehicle so powerful that it, even more completely than in Denham, engulfs the tenor? Donne *means* his figure; it is *exactly* what he meant to say. Johnson would doubtless have seen in what Donne says of himself (the scholastic nullity of his spirit as a consequence of the death of Lucy) something highly improper, if not vicious. I anticipate a later stage of this discussion by remarking that Donne evidently did not "enquire . . . what he should have said or done." He had no predetermined tenor in search of a perspicuous vehicle.

At this point I pass beyond certain considerations suggested by the obscure commentaries on Denham (both Johnson's and my own) into more difficult speculations; here I tread cautiously. I begin to approach directly the uncertain object of this enquiry. Johnson's piety is well-known; his views on Christianity were forthright, uncompromising, and beyond controversy; I do not intend to discuss them here. I will cite two brief paragraphs from the "Life of Waller," concerning the relation of poetry and Christian worship:

Contemplative piety, or the intercourse between God and the human soul, cannot be poetical. Man, admitted to implore the mercy of his Creator, and plead the merits of his Redeemer, is already in a higher state than poetry can confer.

The essence of poetry is invention; such invention as, by producing something unexpected, surprises and delights. The topics of devotion are few, and being few are universally known; but, few as they are, they can be made no more; they receive no grace from novelty of sentiment, and very little from novelty of expression.

There is a certain common sense in these paragraphs, if we read them very freely: Poetry is not religion, or even a substitute for it. But what Johnson actually says is that religious contemplation is not a subject for poetry; and this is nonsense. The first paragraph evinces an ignorance of religious poetry, or an indifference to it, comparable to the incapacity of an American critic three generations later, whose critical style was influenced by Johnson: Edgar Allan Poe. Whether poetry can confer a state either higher or lower than that of contemplative piety becomes a meaningless question if we ask first whether it can *confer* any sort of state. Whether religious experience can be the subject of poetry is another question equally unreal. One does not ask whether a man has two arms and two legs, and expect to deduce the Laputan answer; for he obviously has both. Great devotional poetry obviously exists. (What was Johnson doing with St. John of the Cross, the poems of St. Thomas Aquinas, or even, for that matter, with the Psalms of David?) At the end of Johnson's second paragraph one finds another dubious distinction between sentiment and expression. The sentiment remains unknown without the expression, whether it be "novel" or common. (Johnson's rhetorical parallelism frequently leads him by the nose, into saying more, or something else, than he means.) Whether from novelty of sentiment or of expression it is difficult to see how the "topics" of devotion could receive "grace." No one has ever asserted that they did, unless it be the grace snatched beyond the reach of art. Is this "grace" of the "higher state than poetry" supernatural grace sacramentally conferred? No one has ever asserted that poetry could confer it. Some poems (and their apologists) have asserted that we can get along without it; but that is another problem.

No historical considerations have entered into my rough treatment of Johnson; I am reading him out of his time, in my own time, countering his explicit prejudice with prejudice, perhaps not sufficiently explored, of my own. It would be instructive but beside the point to show that Johnson's strictures upon religious poetry are neo-classical criticism at a level of insight where as literary critic he could turn out the light, and revert to private feelings at a depth untouched by his "positive training." Johnson, like most critics whose philosophical powers are in themselves not impressive (and unlike Coleridge), is at his best when he is reading or comparing texts. If we continue to think of Johnson at his best as a critic with a postive training in the English neo-classical school, we shall understand more sympathetically his insistence that the end of poetry is delight leading to instruction; its means, invention. What he finds wrong with religious poetry is probably the same thing that he finds wrong with Denham. The devotional objects, being "universally known," provide a fixed "tenor" for which no new metaphorical vehicle or invention is adequate or necessary; for only the tenor is "true." Institutional religion is the immense paraphrase, no longer, if ever, seen as resting upon a metaphorical base, of the religious experience. The imaginative act of returning the paraphrase to the hazards of new experience (new vehicles) is an impiety, even a perversity which he reproves in the Metaphysical poets.

The foregoing digression into the quotations from the lives of Denham and Waller has seemed to me necessary in order to form as clear a notion as possible of Johnson's assumptions about metaphor. Nowhere in the "Life of Cowley," which I shall now glance at, shall we find so close a scrutiny of language as his analysis of Denham's couplets, or a limitation upon the province of poetry so clearly defined in ultimate religious terms, as in the paragraphs on Waller. The "Life of Cowley" ends with a formidable string of quotations, none of which receives a thorough going-over. His strictures upon Cowley and

Donne take the form of generalizations from a considerable body of poetry, but like Aristotle on poetic diction he leaves the application to us. I conceive his criticism of the Metaphysicals to be grounded in certain philosophical assumptions of his time about the meaning of Reason and Nature: I have neither competence nor space to deal extensively with such questions. Doubtless the New Learning of the seventeenth century, which Mr. Wimsatt finds typically reflected in Johnson, and the philosophy of Locke, gave a rationalistic tinge to his conceptions of reason and nature, and buttressed his literary neo-classicism and thus his views on the province of poetry.

We must now make what we can of some crucial passages from the "Life of Cowley":

. . . they [the Metaphysical poets] neither copied nature nor life; neither painted the forms of matter nor represented the operations of intellect . . . they were not successful in representing or moving the affections.

They had no regard to that uniformity of sentiment which enables us to conceive and to excite the pains and pleasures of other minds; they never enquired what on any occasion they should have said or done; but wrote rather as beholders than partakers of human nature. . . . Their wish was only to say what had never been said before.

The first of these excerpts contains Johnson's general objection, which could easily take us philosophically far afield. If we roughly equate "nature" with "forms of matter," and "life" with "operations of intellect," we get the solid objects of eighteenth century physics (inorganic: no internal change), and a rationalistic epistemology which orders the objects in fixed relations. I am not able to develop this inference further, but it may be sufficient for my purpose to guess that we have here, in the "operations of intellect" upon the "forms of matter," Locke's secondary qualities in a stable relation to the primary; so that the perception of qualities and discourse about them are a single act of mind. Likewise in Johnson's representation and moving of the affections there is both a perceptual and a cognitive limit beyond which the poet exceeds the known and fixed limits of emotion. Thus the Metaphysical poets failed to enquire into the limits of what can be said; they failed to respect, in ignoring the strict conventions of imitation, the neo-classical standard of generalized emotion, scene, and character; they lacked the uniformity of sentiment which Johnson's positive culture supported. Because they wrote outside the eighteenth century canon they wrote outside, rather than within, human nature.

At this point one should pause to distinguish certain historical differences between the situation of Donne and the old age of English Baroque, when in the 1770's it had passed into Rococo. What little I know about these differences is better known by the scholars in the two fields, though perhaps few scholars know both; I should not in any case wish to rely too much upon terms taken from architecture. And we must not assume that the Rococo artist ought to understand the origins of his style in the Baroque; there is no reason why Johnson should have understood Donne. The age of Johnson had achieved in verse a *period* style. Whatever may have been its remote origins in the age of Donne (it became something very different from its origins), it was a style that we could not write today, and was perhaps inconceivable to Donne and his contemporaries. With the exceptions of Milton (excluding "Lycidas") and Shakespeare, both of whom were so "great" that he could scarcely miss them, he lacked the critical terms and the philosophical temper for the estima-

tion of poetry outside his period style. Perhaps a high development of period style always entails upon its critics a
provincial complacency towards the styles of the past
which have not directly contributed to it (one thinks of
Pound and early Eliot on Milton, both men concerned
about a language for a period); and we get almost inevitably a progressive view of poetry. One of the aims of Johnson's proposed, but never written, History of Criticism
was to give "An Account of the Rise and Improvement of
that Art." But there is no invidious inference to be drawn
from his prospectus; there is no evidence that a bad poet
after Dryden could win his praise.

Whether he preferred Cowley as a forerunner of his own
period style, to Donne, or whether the committee of forty-
three booksellers who underwrote the Lives did not consider Donne a poet of enough "reputation" to justify a
new edition, is a scholar's question; yet it is not without an
answer of the internal sort if we are willing to glance at
Johnson's praise of Cowley's "Of Wit." Of this poem he
says:

The Ode on Wit is almost without a rival. It was about the time
of Cowley that *wit*, which had been till then used for *intellection*, in contra-distinction to *will*, took the meaning, whatever it
be, which it now bears. . . . Of all the passages in which poets
have exemplified their own precepts, none will easily be found
of greater excellence than that in which Cowley condemns ex-
uberance of wit.

He then quotes the fifth stanza, of which we may glance
at these lines:

> Several lights will not be seen,
> If there be nothing else between.
> Men doubt because they stand so thick i' the skie,
> If those be stars which paint the Galaxie.

If this does not exhibit the excess of conceit against which
it was written, then one has wasted one's life in the concern
for poetry (a possibility that must always be kept in view);
but short of facing such a crisis one must regretfully im-
pute to Johnson a lapse of judgment at a moment when his
prejudice is flattered. The passage flatters Johnson otherwise: lines three and four are a couplet that Dryden, in a
fit of absent-mindedness, might have written, and that, but
for the extra syllable in the fifth foot of the third line, could
have been written by Pope in a moment of fatigue.

I have disclaimed any ability to estimate Johnson's specific criticism of the Metaphysical poets; but I seem to have
been judging it, perhaps inevitably; exposition without incidental judgment is not possible. But I now return to the
more neutral enquiry into the contrasting uses of figurative
language, of which Johnson stands for one extreme and
Donne for another. The instructive paragraph for this purpose, in the "Life of Cowley," has not had much attention
from critics of either Johnson or Donne; I quote it entire:

Nor was the sublime more within their reach than the pathetic;
for they never attempted that comprehension and expanse
which at once fills the whole mind, and of which the first effect
is sudden astonishment, and the second rational admiration.
Sublimity is produced by aggregation, littleness by dispersion.
Great thoughts are always general, and consist in positions not
limited by exceptions, and in descriptions not descending to
minuteness. It is with great propriety that subtility, which in its
original import means exility of particles, is taken in its metaphorical meaning for nicety of distinction. Those writers who
lay on the watch for novelty, could have little hope of greatness;
for great things cannot have escaped former observation. *Their
attempts were always analytic; they broke every image into
fragments; and could no more represent, by their slender con-
ceits and laboured particularities, the prospects of nature, or*

*the scenes of life, than he who dissects a sunbeam with a prism
can exhibit the wide effulgence of a summer noon.*

Up to the last sentence of this remarkable pronouncement
about half of the ghost of Longinus is the presiding, if
somewhat equivocal authority. (Longinus did not *oppose*
the "sublime" to the "little.") Great things, even in Johnson's testimony, had escaped former observation before
Shakespeare, and Shakespeare left a few to Pope. But it
is good neo-classical doctrine: "But when t'examine every
part he came, / Nature and Homer were, he found, the
same." It is the doctrine of the Grandeur of Generality
given a critical formula in the phrases "positions not limited
by exceptions" and "descriptions not descending to minuteness." If Mr. Leavis is right in saying that Johnson had little
dramatic sense (he could still have had it and written
Irene), it is a defect that seems general in that age, when
men assumed a static relation between the mind and its
object, between poet and subject. The universals that have
not escaped former observation are again the big tenors
which must not be limited by too many exceptions in the
vehicles: invention is all very well if the poet doesn't mean
it too hard; if he does it will not win rational admiration
for the "minute particulars" in which Blake saw the life
not only of poetry but of the spirit. We can scarcely blame
Johnson if in describing what poetry ought to be he described the weak side of Pope's and his own.

But the remarkable last sentence of the paragraph might
well be set down as the main text of this commentary: I
hope I shall not give it an unfair reading. "Their attempts,"
says Johnson, "were always analytic; they broke every
image into fragments." He asks us to prejudge Cowley and
his fellows before we are given to understand how we
should judge them: it is, generally speaking, bad to *break*

things. What are the "attempts" of the Metaphysicals? Their poems, or isolated figures? I assume that he means this: they used metaphor in such a way as to produce analytic effects; they got inside the object and exhibited it as a collection, or dispersion, of "laboured particularities." I confess that I do not understand what I have just written: I can think of no poem of the Metaphysical school of which Johnson's words or my own gloss would be a just description. One could play with an irresponsible sorites, and take analytic to mean in the Kantian and, for Johnson, anachronistic sense, a predicate containing nothing that is not already in the subject. Johnson would then be censuring the Metaphysicals for having done what he should have praised them for: for giving us "images" the qualities of which were already known. His censure is for the Kantian synthetic judgment; for the Metaphysical flight beyond the predictable character of the object, or for the internal exploration of new imaginative objects not known in the neo-classical properties. Johnson I daresay did not know that he was a neo-classicist; so he boggles at the violation of what he deemed the eternal principles of style discovered by the ancients and rediscovered by his own forerunners for the improvement of English poetry. By analytic I take it that he also meant the assertion of marginal similarities as total, like the lovers-compasses simile which virtually claims an identity on the thin ground that lovers, like compasses, must lean towards each other before they can become the two congruent lines of the embrace. By analytic he means a fragmentation of objects in pursuit of "occult resemblances."

The famous phrase brings us to the even more famous "definition" of Metaphysical poetry, in which it occurs:

But wit, abstracted from its effects upon the hearer, may be more rigorously and philosophically considered as a kind of *discordia concors;* a combination of dissimilar images, or discovery of occult resemblances in things apparently unlike.

One is constantly impressed by Johnson's consistency of point of view, over the long pull of his self-dedication to letters. There is seldom either consistency or precision in his particular judgments and definitions—a defect that perhaps accounts negatively for his greatness as a critic: the perpetual reformulation of his standards, with his eye on the poetry, has done much to keep eighteenth century verse alive in our day. His theories (if his ideas ever reach that level of logical abstraction) are perhaps too simple for our taste and too improvised; but his reading is disciplined and acute. There is no doubt that the definition of Metaphysical wit is an improvisation of terms, but it represents the result of long and sensitive meditation on a body of verse which he could not like but the importance of which he had to acknowledge. A brief scrutiny of this definition turns up the astonishing metaphor of sound, *discordia concors,* coming after the promise to give us not a psychological but an epistemological view of wit. We were to have got what wit is, not how it affects us. I don't want to quibble about this matter; I want to emphasize the essential accuracy of one of the great critical insights. It is a new insight based upon a long critical tradition going back to the *Poetics* (Chapter 22):

It is a great thing indeed to make a proper use of these poetical forms, as also of compounds and strange words. But the greatest thing by far is to be a master of metaphor. It is the one thing that cannot be learned from others; and it is also a sign of genius, since a good metaphor implies an intuitive perception of the similarity in dissimilars.

It would have been helpful in the past twenty-three hundred years if Aristotle had told us what a good metaphor is, and settled the matter. How far should the perception of similarity go? The *Poetics* seems to be a fragment, and we shall not get Aristotle's wisdom (if he had it) for our folly. We have Johnson's, in the second sentence after the quotation above; and he writes what is possibly his best descriptive criticism of the Metaphysical style:

The most heterogeneous ideas are yoked by violence together. . . .

By what kind of violence? A poetry of violence may have its own validity in its own time, and even for other times. Again we confront Johnson's point of view done up in an approximate generalization, which for all its heuristic accuracy begs the question which it conceals. The question is how much violence is allowable, and at what point does the yoking of dissimilars in similarity overreach itself and collapse under the strain?[2] It would be critical folly to decide how much stretch Johnson would allow, a folly of which he was happily not guilty. The allowed stretch is the stretch of one's age (with one eye on other ages), the tensions within the religious and moral struggle that the poet must acknowledge in himself.

If we may reasonably get around this defeating relativism, what direction shall we take? One direction is towards the chasm; to the leap into the unhistorical and timeless generalization of the late Paul Valéry; but only sceptics who believe in unicorns had better travel that road. Another road leads to the Palace of Wisdom where

2. Mr. Samuel H. Monk has called my attention to a passage in the "Life of Addison" which I had overlooked: "A simile may be compared to lines converging at a point, and is more excellent as the lines approach from greater distance: an exemplification may be considered as two parallel lines which run together without approximation, never far separated, and never joined." This is itself an excellent simile, but its tenor has whatever degree of obscurity one may find in "distance." It would abstractly make room for Donne's wildest figures; but Johnson could still reply that these seldom "converge."

there aren't any poets; and criticism may want in the end to get along without poetry. Between the chasm and the feather bed (Mr. Blackmur's version of the Palace of Wisdom), somewhere between the down and the up, lies the region that most critics inhabit without quite knowing where it is. That is not too desperate an ignorance, if one remembers that Poe was Valéry's unicorn (desperate scepticism indeed) and that autotelism is usually a bed of feathers that no longer sing. I am not confident that Johnson would like this mixture of feathers, a Palace, and a unicorn; and I am not sure that he would not be right.

Nor can I be sure that his failure to understand Donne as we think we understand him was a real failure. I have concealed the questions I have put to him, as he concealed his, by begging them. One would prefer to *note down,* as dispassionately as possible, his dogmatic rejection of all religious poetry which is not pietistic or devotional; his static psychology of perception; his fixed natural order; his fixed decorum in diction. It all adds up to a denial of validity to what in our age has been called a poetry of experience. A poetry of experience is incipiently a poetry of action; hence of drama, the sense of which Johnson seems to have lacked. The minute particulars of the wrestling with God, which we find in Donne and Crashaw, bring the religious experience into the dimension of immediate time. Johnson's implied division of poetry into the meditative and the descriptive (implied also in his own verse) fixes its limits, arresting the subject within the frame of pictorial space: *ut pictura poesis*, for his typical *period* verb for the poetic effect is that the poet *paints*. The breaking up of the image, of which he accuses the Metaphysical poets, is the discovery of a dynamic relation between the mind and its objects, in a poetry which does not recognize the traditional topic; the subject becomes the metaphorical structure, it is no longer the set theme. The ideas that re-sult from the dynamic perception of objects (language it-self is thus an object) are in constant disintegration; so in-ferentially are the objects themselves. The "object" which poetry like "The Extasie" or "The Canonization" suggests that we locate, is not an existence in space, but an essence created by the junction of the vehicle and the tenor of the leading metaphor. It is not *in* space; it moves with experi-ence in time.

As I come to a close I am aware of a certain provincialism of amateur metaphysics, as well as of some critical impre-cision, in the foregoing remarks; and I am not sure that I have not had in mind the poetry of our age a little more fully than the poetry of the age of Donne; that my own core of prejudice has not been witlessly revealed. That preju-dice, if it is more than private, would run as follows: the great tradition of modern verse unites Shakespeare and Donne, includes Milton and much of Dryden, but passes over the eighteenth century until the year 1798. This is not to say that Dryden was a greater poet than Pope, though he may have been; it is rather to say that the neo-classical age was an interlude between modernisms, that it had by-passed the Renaissance Nature of *depth* and re-stored the classical Nature of *surface*. But the *Prelude* brought us back: to the breakup of the solid object in the dynamic stream of time.

That the poets may have cracked the atom before the physicists gives us the dubious pride of discovery; but I daresay few persons feel any pride in some of the more practical results. The neo-classical age died because it could not move; we may be dying because we cannot stop moving. Our poetry has become process, including its own processes. It is pleasant to remember Aristotle's summary treatment of metaphor and his elaborate description of the structure of the greatest of the genres. Were not the genres so powerful, so nearly rooted in nature herself, that their languages could be taken for granted? They would last forever. Poetic diction could be brought under arithmetical rules of thumb; it was nicely settled in its relation to the wonderful collection of solid objects scattered through space; it could never be a problem in itself. Into that space time entered not as process but as myth. It is not a question which is the better view to look down at, the classical or ours; one may not choose one's view if one expects to see anything. I end these remarks on two uses of figurative language with the observation that I have not taken them further than I did in a recent essay on Longinus. But I have taken them as far as I am able; perhaps further.

8

Longinus and the
"New Criticism"[1]

To BEGIN an essay with a silent apology to the subject is commendable, but one should not expect the reader to be interested in it. I allude to the ignorance in which I had underestimated Longinus, before I reread him after twenty years, because I am convinced that it is typical. Who reads Longinus? I do not mean to say literally that he is not read. There is an excellent recent study by Mr. Elder Olson; there are the fine books by Mr. T. R. Henn and Mr. Samuel H. Monk,[1] which persons of the critical interest should know something about and doubtless do. Until these books appeared, there had been no serious consideration of Longinus since Saintsbury's A History of Criticism (1900). In some twenty-five years of looking at criticism in the United States and England, I have not seen, with the exceptions already noticed, a reference to the περὶ ὕψους which is of more than historical interest. One might, with misplaced antiquarian zeal, find the name, if not much more, of Aristotle in the pages of a fashionable journal like

1. T. R. Henn: Longinus and English Criticism (Cambridge, 1934); and Samuel H. Monk: The Sublime: A Study of Critical Theories in XVIII-Century England (New York, 1935).

Horizon; one would have to go to the learned journals,
which few critics see, to find even the name of Longinus.
Until Mr. Henn and Mr. Monk reminded us of him, he
had been dropped out of active criticism since the end of
the eighteenth century. I should like to believe that these
excellent scholars have brought about a Longinian revival.
Mr. Herbert Read informs me that Coleridge in *Table Talk*
spoke of him as "no very profound critic." It must seem to
us today that Coleridge buried him in that remark. I am
not confident that I shall succeed where Mr. Monk and Mr.
Henn failed (if they did fail), that what I am about to say
will exhume Longinus.

I

This is not the occasion to establish a correct English title
for περὶ ὕψους. (In the New Testament ὕψος means not the
physical heavens [οὐρανός] but something like "on high.")
To my mind, the idea of height or elevation contained in
the title, *Of the Height of Eloquence,* which was given to
the work by the first English translator, John Hall, in 1652,
is more exact than *On the Sublime,* which carries with it
the accretions of Boileau and the English eighteenth century, and the different meanings contributed later by
Burke and Kant, which are far removed from anything
that I have been able to find in this third- (or is it first- ?)
century treatise. So far from Kant's is Longinus' conception of "sublimity" that one pauses at the marvelous se-
mantic history of the word. In Chapter IX Longinus quotes
a passage from the *Iliad,* Book XX, about the war of the
gods, and comments: "Yet these things terrible as they are,
if they are not taken as an allegory are altogether blasphemous and destructive of what is seemly." To allegorize infinite magnitude, quantity beyond the range of the eye, is
to reduce it to the scale of what Kant called the Beautiful

as distinguished from the Sublime. The "sublimity" of the passage, in the Kantian sense, Longinus could not accept. These shifts of meaning are beyond the scope of my interest and my competence. Three other brief and confusing parallels will fix in our minds the difficulties of Longinus' title. His insight, perhaps unique in antiquity, which is contained in the distinction between the "persuasion" of oratory and the "transport" of what, for want of a better phrase, one may call the literary effect, reappears in this century as neo-symbolism and surrealism. Some twenty years ago the Abbé Bremond decided that "transport" meant religious mysticism, and wrote a book called *La Poésie pure*. In England, about thirty years ago, Arthur Machen, of whom few people of the generations younger than mine have heard, the author of *The Hill of Dreams* and other novels after Huysmans, wrote a small critical book called *Hieroglyphics*. Machen proposed to discern the real thing in literature with a test that he called "ecstasy," but what made Machen ecstatic left many persons cold. At any rate, the Greek word in Longinus that we translate as "transport" is ἔκστασις. Had Boileau not stuffed Longinus with neo-classical "authority," would he have been discovered by the French and English romantics, to whom he could have spoken from another if equally wrong direction? This topic may be dropped with the observation that literary history is no more orderly than any other history.

I shall, then, in the following remarks, think of the two key terms in Longinus, ὕψος and ἔκστασις, as respectively Elevation of Language and Transport; but I cannot expect to disentangle them from each other. They contain, in their interrelations, a version of a persistent ambiguity of critical reference which appeared with Aristotle, had vigorous life up to Coleridge (with whom it comes back disguised), and now eggs on an edifying controversy of the contemporary

English and American critics: Ransom, Cleanth Brooks, Read, Leavis, Richards, Blackmur, and Winters. Is Elevation an objective quality of the literary work? Is Transport its subjective reference denoting the emotions of the reader —or the "hearer," as Longinus calls him—as he receives the impact of Elevation? Does either word, Elevation or Transport, point to anything sufficiently objective to be isolated for critical discussion?

This is not the moment to answer that question, if I were competent to answer it. Our first duty is to find out how Longinus asks it. After defining Elevation tautologically, in Chapter I, as "a kind of supreme excellence of discourse" (ἐξοχή τις λόγων ἐστὶ τὰ ὕψη), he describes its effect:

For what is out of the common affects the hearer not to persuade but to entrance (οὐ γὰρ εἰς πειθὼ τοὺς ἀκροωμένους ἀλλ᾿ εἰς ἔκστασιν ἄγει τὰ ὑπερφυᾶ). It moves to wonder and surprise, and always wins against what is merely delightful or persuasive. It is not enough in one or two passages of a work to exhibit invention schooled by experience, nor again the fine order and distribution of its parts, nor even these qualities displayed throughout. Rather, I suggest, does the sublime, fitly expressed, pierce everything like a flash of lightning. . . .[2]

Not to persuade, but to entrance, like a flash of lightning. In these words Longinus breaks with the rhetoricians who had dominated ancient criticism since Aristotle, four to six hundred years before him, and who continued to dominate it until the seventeenth century. Neither Longinus nor Dante, in De Vulgari Eloquentia, had any influence on critical theory after them, until the time of Boileau, when

2. With the exception of a few phrases I quote throughout from the translation by Frank Granger (London, 1935), which seems to me the most perspicuous English version. The exceptions are the result of a collation of the Granger and other versions with what is probably the definitive scholarly translation, by W. Rhys Roberts (Cambridge, 1899). All the modern translations render ὕψος as "sublime," and it has obviously been necessary to keep the word when it occurs in a quoted passage.

Longinus was used to justify rules that he had never made. Dante's criticism has languished in the department of biography; at best, in the history of criticism, as a document of the time.

II

Chapter II opens with the question: "We must first discuss whether there is an art of the sublime." In the Greek, the phrase is ὕψους τις ἤ βάθους τέχνη—"an art of height or of depth"; but the word we should attend is τέχνη, "art," which the Greeks used for any teachable skill, from metal-working to music and medicine. They applied the term to all the skills of making for which an objective rationale could be devised. Longinus explains the views of Caecilius, the opponent of uncertain identity whom the περὶ ὕψους was written to refute, who believed that elevation of language came through nature alone, that the great writer, born great, needs nothing but his birth. In this controversy of lively acrimony with a man who may have been dead three hundred years (such was the leisure of antiquity), Longinus at the beginning of his essay opposes, in opposing Caecilius, both the Platonic and the Aristotelian doctrines, and holds that style is a compound of natural talent and conscious method. He thus parts with Plato's "divine madness" in the *Ion*, and implicitly claims for Thought and Diction, two of the nonstructural elements in Aristotle's analysis of tragedy, a degree of objectivity that Aristotle's rhetorical view of poetic language could not include.

If literary method cannot alone produce a style, the judgment of which, says Longinus, "is the last fruit of long experience," it can "help us to speak at the right length and to the occasion." How much interpretation of a casual observation such as this, which is only common sense, the modern scholiast is entitled to develop, I do not know. Although Longinus may have in mind merely the orator and the *public* occasion, may we just see him reaching out for a criterion of objectivity for any sort of literary composition? The "right length" is the adaptation of form to subject; and is not the "occasion" the relation between the poet and the person to whom the poem is addressed? We have, foreshadowed here, I think, a principle of dramatic propriety, a sense of the "point of view" in composition, the prime literary strategy which can never be made prescriptive, but which exhibits its necessity equally in its operation and in its lapse. Later, discussing meter, Longinus tells us that Elevation cannot be achieved in the trochaic, or tripping, meter, and we may dismiss the remark as the perennial fallacy which identifies certain fixed effects with certain meters. But if we can imagine "Lycidas" written in trochees and "The Raven" in iambuses, we might suppose the one would be worse, the other considerably better. And if we look at "length" and "occasion" in somewhat different terms, we shall find ourselves again in the thick of one of our own controversies. Does not the occasion force upon the poet the objective and communicable features of his work? Are they not Mr. Winters' theory of the relation of "feeling" to "rational content" and Mr. Ransom's theory of a "texture" within a "structure"?

In exceeding the literal text of Longinus in this matter, I hope that I have not also stretched two living critics into an agreement which they have scarcely acknowledged; nor should I ask them to acknowledge Longinus as their forerunner. I suggest that Longinus' question "Is there an art of Elevation?" is the question we are asking today, somewhat as follows: can there be a criticism of convincing objectivity which approaches the literary work through the analysis of style and which arrives at its larger aspects through that aperture?

That is the question of our time. In asking it, are we not following Longinus rather than Aristotle? Aristotle began with the conspicuous "larger aspects" of a mature literary genre, Greek tragedy, and got around to the problems of poetic language only at the end, and as a rhetorician (except for one curious remark about metaphor) who offers us shrewd but merely schematic advice about the use of figures.

III

If there is an art of Elevation, if there is possible a coherent criticism of literature through its language, it follows that we must examine good and bad writers together, in order to arrive, not at rules, but at that "judgment of style which is the fruit of long experience"; to arrive at that sense of the length and the occasion which will permit us, as poets, to imitate not Homer's style but its excellence, in our own language. It is here that intensive literary criticism and literary tradition work together; it is here that we arrive at the idea of a literary tradition which does not enjoin the slavery of repetition, but the emulation which comes of insight. We shall have of course to deal as best we can with the ambiguity of Longinus' word τέχνη. By the "art of height or of depth" does he mean criticism? Or does he mean the "art" of the poet? He means, I take it, both; and it is proper that he should. For our sense of the achievement of the past may issue in a critical acquisition of knowledge which is not to be put away in the attic when the creative moment comes. At this point one may profitably notice two characteristic defects, defects of its quality, that proud and self-sufficient writers fall into in attempting the elevated style. "Frigidity," says Longinus, is the over-elaboration of the academic writer, a violation of length due to aiming at "the curious and the artificial." The "feeling" (or the detail) is unreal in the sense that it is on a scale smaller than its intelligible form. Likewise, the opposite fault—and in describing it Longinus has written as good criticism as any I know—of Thomas Wolfe and the contemporary lyrical novel; he says:

Theodorus calls it the mock-inspired. It is emotion out of place and empty where there is no need of it, or lack of proportion where proportion is needed. Some writers fall into a maudlin mood and digress from their subject into their own tedious emotion. Thus they show bad form and leave their audience unimpressed: necessarily, for they are in a state of rapture, and the audience is not.

If this is the performance of the writer great by nature and beyond "art," Henry James gives us his dreary portrait: "The writer who cultivates his instinct rather than his awareness sits by finally in a stale and shrinking puddle." His awareness of what? I should say of the "occasion" and the "length," the sense of limiting structure and of what, within that limit, is to be objectively communicated and made known. This sense becomes operative through "art," τέχνη, technique, the controlled awareness *through* language of what can be made actual *in* language, resulting in a just, if unpredictable, proportion between what Longinus calls the "emotion" and the "subject." Doubtless, any experienced reader of literature can point to the failures of great writers in the two extremes of disproportion corresponding to two forms of pride that prevent the complete discovery of the subject: the pride of intellect and the pride of feeling, the pride of will and the pride of instinct. (Perhaps the history of the imagination is the pendulum between these extremes.) Mr. Blackmur has shown us in the past few years how the thesis in Dostoevsky distorts or even wrecks the theme, the imaginative actuality in which the form ought to have been discovered under pressure of

its internal necessity. In a more recent writer, D. H. Lawrence, we get both extremes of pride: the attack on the intellect in behalf of instinct, instinct itself hardening into a
core of abstraction which operates as intellectual pride, as
thesis; not as realized form.

The instances of "disproportion" could be multiplied,
but I pause to remark my own disgression, and to ask, as
the eighteenth-century critics seem not to have done,
whether there is not already, in what I have said, a certain
excess of gloss, commentary cut loose from the text com-
mented upon, a self-indulgence which seems to attribute
to Longinus a comprehension which one is covertly
claiming for oneself? Criticism should no doubt observe
the same proprieties of occasion and length that we require of the imagination; but it has seldom done so, and
I think with good reason. If criticism is only secondary to
literature, it is thus the dependent partner, and for the
hazards that it must face in every generation it must constantly worry the past for support, and make too much of
what it revives, or perhaps even make it into something
different. Perhaps I have got out of the περὶ ὕψους at this
stage of the discussion only a general insight available, if
not always used, as common property since Coleridge. Yet
we should remember that Longinus alone seems to have
achieved it in the ancient world.

I have been trying to see the outlines, before I move on
to some of the particular judgments in the περὶ ὕψους, of a
possible framework into which to put Longinus' profound
but topical dialectic. In the same chapter (II) in which the
proportions of length and occasion are held to be established through "art" or method, he writes this crucial
passage:

Demosthenes says somewhere that in ordinary life luck is the
greatest good, and that it cannot exist without another which is

not inferior to it, namely prudent conduct. Following him, we might say, in the case of style, that nature takes the place of good luck; and art, of prudent conduct. *Most important of all, we must learn from art the fact that some elements of style depend upon nature alone.*

At this point four pages of the manuscript disappear, a loss of the first importance to critical theory. If the amateur Hellenist reads from classical criticism a passage in which the word "nature" occurs, he is likely to read it with Boileau or the English eighteenth century, and get entangled in the thickets of "nature," which they opposed to "art," when they were not effecting a compromise by making art nature to advantage dressed; and so on. It seems to me that we ought to support the passage just quoted with a full sense of the special kind of judgment that Longinus brings to bear upon the actual texture of Greek literature; he produces many examples which cannot be cited here. We could then just see in it the first declaration of independence from the practical, forensic eloquence of the rhetoricians.

"Most important of all, we must learn from art the fact that some elements of style depend upon nature alone." In trying to understand this nice oxymoron, I shall take risks which are perhaps not greater than those taken by most commentators on the *Poetics*. Most important of all, I make Longinus say, we learn from the development of technique that stylistic autonomy is a delusion, because style comes into existence only as it discovers the subject; and conversely the subject exists only after it is formed by the style. No literary work is perfect, no subject perfectly formed. Style reveals that which is not style in the process of forming it. Style does not create the subject, it discovers it. The fusion of art and nature, of technique and subject, can never exceed the approximate; the margin of imperfection, of the unformed, is always there—nature intractable to art, art unequal to nature. The converse of Longinus' aphorism will further elucidate it: we must learn from nature that some elements of subject matter, in a literary work, "depend" upon art alone. There is a reciprocal relation, not an identity—not, certainly, the identity of form and content—a dynamic, shifting relation between technique and subject; and they reveal each other. This is my sense of Longinus' primary insight. It is an insight of considerable subtlety that has a special claim to the attention of our generation.

IV

I suppose we should agree that by and large the critical method of the *Poetics* is inductive. Aristotle's generalizations proceed from a scrutiny of one kind of literature, drama, chiefly from one kind of drama, tragedy, and from one kind of tragedy, Greek. Longinus repeats Aristotle's animadversions on "character," which Aristotle seems to think need not be much developed if the "plot" is good. We must constantly remind ourselves of the narrow range of literature at the command of the two great critics of antiquity; they lacked the novel, for one thing, and Aristotle evidently did not consider the works of his great predecessor and teacher worthy of the name of "poetry." The larger conception of *literature* does not appear in the *Poetics*. Although Longinus, trained as he must have been in the rhetorical schools, did not see clearly whither he was heading, it is just the awareness of *literature at large* which raises his theory of the relation of language and subject to a higher degree of useful generality than any literary theory before him had reached. He is the first, though necessarily incomplete, literary critic. His question, put again, in its wider implications, is: what distinguishes literature from practical oratory, from history? A quality, he says in effect, beyond an immediate purpose. His discussion of imagination is what we should expect: it is the classical rhetorician's view of the image as a "mental picture," which he, along with his age, seems to believe must be laid on the work discreetly from the top. Yet the distinction between two widely different purposes in the controlled use of language puts his doctrine on a high yet accessible level of empirical generalization, and makes it possible for him to look beyond specific conventions to estimate the value of a literature offering a great variety of forms and structures.

It has been supposed by many critics that Longinus is not interested in structure, that his doctrine of "transport" and the "lightning flash" anticipates the romantic *frisson*, or that Pope did it justice when he called in Longinus to help him "snatch a grace beyond the reach of art." I think I have shown that Longinus would reject that art which is beyond its own reach. And what, in fact, I now wish to show is that Longinus is quite prepared to put his finger directly upon the problem of structure, and by implication to tell us that structure is not in the formal "type" or genre, a viable body of special conventions, such as the lyric, the ode, or the epic provides, but exists in the language of the poem.

After discussing, in Chapters VIII and IX, the five sources of Elevation in language (to which I shall return), he analyzes the effect, from the point of view of structure, of Sappho's Ode to Anactoria, beginning: φαίνεταί μοι κῆνος ἴσος θεοῖσιν. The analysis is brief (everything in Longinus is brief but the lacunae in the text), yet it is probably the first example in criticism of structural analysis of a lyric poem. (I ought for my purpose here to know more than I do, which is virtually nothing, about the ancient theory of the Passions.) I quote the entire passage:

Let us now go on to see whether we have anything further by means of which we can raise our words to the sublime. Since, then, in the substance of everything, we find certain elements which naturally belong to it, we should of course find one cause of the sublime by always choosing the most relevant circumstances and by compounding them (ἐπισυνθέσει) to make, so to speak, one body (ἕν τι σῶμα ποιεῖν). For the audience is attracted, first by our choice of topics (ὁ μὲν γὰρ τῇ ἐκλογῇ . . . τῶν λημμάτων), and second, by the conciseness of our exposition. For example, Sappho takes from their actual setting the feelings that accompany the frenzy of love. Where then does she display her skill? In the tact with which she chooses and binds together supreme and intense feelings.

> Peer of Gods he seemeth to me, the blissful
> Man who sits and gazes at thee before him,
> Close beside thee sits, and in silence hears thee
>   Silverly speaking,
>
> Laughing love's low laughter. Oh this, this only
> Stirs the troubled heart in my breast to tremble!
> For should I but see thee a little moment,
>   Straight is my voice hushed;
>
> Yea, my tongue is broken, and through and through me
> 'Neath the flesh impalpable fire runs tingling;
> Nothing see mine eyes, and a noise of roaring
>   Waves in my ear sounds;
>
> Sweat runs down in rivers, a tremor seizes
> All my limbs, and paler than grass in autumn,
> Caught by pains of menacing death, I falter,
>   Lost in the love trance. . . .

Do you not wonder how she gives chase at once to soul and body, to words and tongue, to sight and color, all as if scattered abroad, how *uniting contradictions*,[3] she is frozen and burns, she raves and is wise? For either she is panic-stricken or at point of death; she is haunted not by a single emotion but their *whole company*.[4]

Towards the end of the περὶ ὕψους there is some scattered commentary on the rhetorical figures; but in the criticism of Sappho the language is not that of the tropes and figures. In so far as it concerns emotion, it is "psychological," if not very exact, even in the terms of the classical psychology of the passions; yet perhaps it is not too much to claim for Longinus' perception of opposites in this poem, of the positive compulsion given tension by its negative, that it goes deeper and is more attentive to what the poem says than anything that Arnold has to say about Keats' or Milton's poetry. *He is trying to see what is happening in the poem.* If he is hampered by his affective terms, so was Mr. T. S. Eliot when, in an early essay, he was getting at a similar play of opposites (what Mr. Cleanth Brooks has since called "paradox") by proposing his theory of the "positive" and the "negative" emotion, and more especially the theory of the central "emotion" gathering up and controlling a variety of contingent "feelings." Mr. Eliot's early theory I should call advanced romantic criticism: it was struggling through the subjective effect towards the objective structure of the work. Longinus' criticism of Sappho is advanced romantic criticism, as advanced as Mr. Eliot's.

3. I have inserted here W. Rhys Roberts' translation of καθ' ὑπεναντιώσεις because it conveys more accurately the force of the Greek, which means *opposite feelings* rather than "at variance within," as Granger has it.

4. Roberts has it "a concourse of passions," which is more accurate. The Greek ἵνα μὴ ἕν τι περὶ αὐτὴν πάθος φαίνηται, παθῶν δὲ σύνοδος is literally a "coming together of roads," a crossroads; so better perhaps than either "their whole company" or a "concourse of passions" are the renditions "a clash of feelings", "a crossing of feelings."

LONGINUS AND THE "NEW CRITICISM"

One hesitates to present to Longinus a theory which I hope is not implicit in his phrase ἕν τι σῶμα ποιεῖν, "to make into one body"; it looks like an organic theory of poetry, but if we suppose that he is merely using the phrase analogically, and means by it no more than he means a moment later, when he says that the poem is a result of choosing and binding together intense feelings, we shall have to acknowledge the presence of a quite modern piece of criticism. At the least, he is telling us that in this poem contradictions are united, bound together, not that Sappho was expressing herself. We are a long step on the way to that critical moment when the affective vocabulary goes over into linguistic analysis, when, instead of what the poem "feels like," we try to decide what it says. That Longinus was farther along this road than we may at a glance suspect there is evidence in the remarkable sentence that he plumps down before us without explanation: ". . . the sublime is often found where there is no emotion." There will be something to say about this when we come to the discussion of "harmony," or composition.

V

The promise at the beginning of the treatise to produce the elements of an Art of Elevation leads to a good deal of miscellaneous specification, under five heads, for its achievement; but the dialectical links among the categories are not distinct. If we think of Longinus as Pascal's man of *finesse,* man of insights, and of Aristotle as a man of *géométrie,* man of deduction, we shall have to look twice at Mr. Olson's observation that, "Unlike Edmund Burke, who finds the sources of sublimity in qualities of the subject matter of art, Longinus finds them in the faculties of the author." This is partly true; but it is misleading, if we

[145]

are led to suppose that Longinus tried but failed to erect a systematic philosophy of art, comparable to Burke's *A Philosophical Enquiry into the Origins of Our Ideas of the Sublime and Beautiful,* but placing the origin of the ideas in the author. He is ambiguous at this point, but I have shown, I hope, that his considerable originality consists in shifting the center of critical interest, without rejecting it as an "interest," from the genetic and moral judgment to the aesthetic, from the subject matter and the psychology of the author to the language of the work. When he describes the first of his five sources of Elevation as the "impulse towards what is great in thought," he speaks perhaps as a casual Platonist, but primarily as a rhetorician in the great tradition reaching from Aristotle to Cicero.

In distinguishing a critical insight from the intellectual discipline from which, to an extent, it may be a departure, we tend to assume that the insight has replaced the discipline; whereas it may merely alter it. It is not certain that we need a philosophical aesthetics in order to produce a work of art; at the Renaissance, I need hardly to observe, an education in rhetoric and oratory produced poets. Sidney is not too apologetic for "straying from Poetrie to Oratorie"; for, he says, "both have such an affinity in this wordish consideration. . . ." It was the point of view of his age. Disciplining that point of view was the art of rhetoric, one member of a tripartite whole completed by ethics and politics; rhetoric was the ethics of the public man in its appropriate discipline, the art of the enthymeme, or rhetorical syllogism.

The second of Longinus' categories, "strong and inspired emotion," proceeds from the first, or from a common source; it also is "due to nature." Here we come upon a curious and, as usual, undeveloped observation. Strong and inspired emotion is one source of, but it is not the same as, style. Pity, grief, and fear, he says, are "humble [ταπεινά: lowly, mean] and without the note of the Sublime"—as if in "pity" and "fear" he had a critical eye to Aristotle, whose doctrine of *katharsis* was practical and even "sociological." The curious observation honors the critic who puts "awareness" above system, for it enters an exception to the rule: "The masters of panegyric," Longinus says, "are seldom given to emotion." What, then, are they given to? An English instance will be helpful. The epigraph to "Lycidas" tells us that "The Author bewails a Learned Friend"—but the author does nothing of the sort;[5] the strong feeling is directed at the clergy, and even it is sufficiently assimilated into the rich pastoral texture.

I pass over sources two and three, the "framing of rhetorical figures" and "nobility of expression," with the remark that Longinus is prudential, like a good teacher, and on these topics not more rewarding than the rhetoricians, Demetrius and Dionysius. But number five, "Composition and distribution of words and phrases into a dignified and exalted unit," heads up the entire argument. "It is a unity of composition," he says, "attained through language." If it is so attained, it is not attained, though it may originate, in the inaccessible nobility of the author's mind. Observe again the superiority of Longinus' insight, with the specific work in mind, to his critical apparatus, which tends to the moralistic and academic. We may see composition here as *ordonnance*, "the best words in the best order." It is more than that. Composition is the total work, not the superaddition of method. Its effect is not to persuade but to entrance; it is "out of the common," not uncommon words, but words used uncommonly well. It is clear that Longinus, by and large, is not recommending the "grand style"; his

5. Mr. John Crowe Ransom made this observation in "A Poem Nearly Anonymous," *The World's Body* (Scribner, 1938), pp. 1-28.

translators have probably done him a disservice in rendering his characteristic adjective μέγα as "grand"; it is, rather, great, unusual, *uncommon;* and likewise ὕψος, "height," which I understand as "excellence." ἔκστασις is our subjective acknowledgement of the presence of the uncommon, of an objective order of unpredictable distinction. He is quite explicit in this matter. By means of "an appropriate *structure,* and by this means only, as we have sufficiently shown, the best writers give the effect of stateliness and distinction which is removed from the commonplace." In illustration he quotes a line from the *Hercules Furens* of Euripides:

γέμω κακῶν δὴ κοὐκετ' ἔσθ' ὅποι τεθῇ,

I am loaded with sorrows nor can I take on more.
"The phrase is quite commonplace but it has *gained elevation* by the arrangement of the words." The fine statement that follows ought to remove any remaining misconception of the nature of "transport," if we still suppose it to be the romantic shudder; it addresses itself to the whole mind:

. . . if a work of literature fails to disclose to the reader's intelligence an outlook beyond the range of what is said, when it dwindles under a careful and continuous inspection, it cannot be truly sublime, for it has reached the ear alone. . . . For that is truly grand [μέγα] of which the contemplation bears repeating.

There must be, in short, a total quality of the work which abides its first impact; to that total quality he gives the name of composition.

It includes rhythm. Saintsbury, whose exposition of Longinus might have revived his influence had somebody else written it, misses the originality of Longinus' treatment of this subject. Longinus' location of rhythm in the total composition, as binding and bound up with it, is perhaps the best critical insight of its kind before Coleridge. Quoting a passage from Demosthenes, he makes the experiment of adding a syllable, and observes that the "sublime phrase is loosened and undone by lengthening of the final rhythm." Likewise, if the phrase were shortened by a syllable. His principle of prose rhythm is negatively stated, but it seems to me to hold for every kind of writing. It is: prose rhythm should not have "a conspicuous movement of sound." It must seem, even if metaphysically it is not, at one with the meaning; it must not call attention to itself, unless—as in Tacitus, Gibbon, Doughty, or Sir Thomas Browne—the "conspicuous movement of sound" is a tonal vehicle that once established is not distinguishable from, but is a part of, the subject itself. But if it is a rhythm "like that of a dancer taking his step before the audience," which the audience anticipates, it distracts attention from what is being said to who is saying it. It is a disproportion in composition similar to that of the orator or the poet who "digresses from the subject into his own tedious emotions." Had Longinus been discussing the rhythm of verse, I should have been able to cite Swinburne and *The Age of Anxiety* by Mr. W. H. Auden.

VI

I have postponed consideration of the third source of Elevation to this concluding section because it pertains in part to metaphor, the *pons asinorum* of literary criticism. If on this subject Longinus is unsatisfactory, it is only a matter of degree; here everybody is unsatisfactory, even Mr. I. A. Richards, whose *Philosophy of Rhetoric* offers a good deal but promises too much. This is a field of inquiry of a difficulty equal to that of the burden of the mystery. Here again Longinus is prudential, but he no doubt gives us as good an account as any of the classical precept of nothing-too-much. Don't use too many metaphors, unless you are overwhelmed by emotions which may make them credible. Follow Aristotle, perhaps in the *Rhetoric;* soften the metaphor up by inserting "as if" or "just as though" and making it a simile that does not assert improbable identities.

One goes through the περὶ ὕψους, and then the *Rhetoric,* half-heartedly and vainly, looking for something better than this, from the literary point of view, that Longinus might have overlooked, or for something as far-reaching as Aristotle's own Delphic pronouncement in Chapter XXII of the *Poetics,* where he says:

It is a great thing indeed to make a proper use of these poetical forms, as also of compounds and strange words. But the greatest thing by far is to be a master of metaphor. It is the one thing that cannot be learnt from others; and it is also a sign of genius, since a good metaphor implies an intuitive perception of the similarity in dissimilars.

That is very nearly the beginning and the end of our own inquiries into metaphor; but I am rash enough to question whether Aristotle, as a Greek, could know, as we have known since Shakespeare and Donne, how similar dissimilars can be made to seem, or (to take an extreme view which is not unknown today) how similar they can be made to *be.* Metaphor, says Aristotle, is the transference of names, through the permutations of genus and species, or by analogy. Metaphor by analogy takes the formula of arithmetical proportion, a quantitative and relational procedure. We are thus in the Greek Cosmos, an ordering of solid objects under a physics of motion, in which the formal object offers but a narrow margin of analogy to any other. If the ancient inquiry into the structure of metaphor was less resourceful than ours, it was not I daresay because

LONGINUS AND THE "NEW CRITICISM"

Aristotle was less intelligent than the best modern critics. Our multiverse has increasingly, since the seventeenth century, consisted of unstable objects dissolving into energy; and there has been no limit to the extension of analogy. Criticism follows whatever it is given to follow. Are the famous lucidity and the restraint of the Greeks evidence that by nature they were more lucid and more restrained than we? I doubt it. For even the physical sight may be controlled by the religious selectivity, which fixes the height and the direction of the casement framing our inspection of the world. To introduce at the end of an essay so large and so undeveloped a conception is an impropriety of length and occasion; I offer it as historical relativism in defense of Longinus and of ourselves.

On no single kind of literature is Longinus as searching as Aristotle on tragedy. But I risk the guess that he came nearer to a comprehensive theory of literary form than any other ancient critic. If he did not quite make the leap to a complete theory of the language of imagination, we must remember that nobody in the ancient world did. He shared Aristotle's sense of the simple relation between word and thing; in a world of fixed forms, thing was unyielding; the word, like its object, retained a plastic visibility. With the Greeks the "transference" of "names" was limited to the surface designation, to the comparison of objects in the round, to sculpturesque analogy. Metaphor was a feature of discourse to be described, not a metaphysical problem to be investigated. We need not see as a critical limitation Longinus' failure to investigate a problem that for him did not exist. The permanent critics do not settle the question. They compel us to ask it again. They are the rotating chairmen of a debate only the rhetoric of which changes from time to time. Among these we may think of Longinus, if we will read him not in our age, but in his own.

[151]

9

A Miscellany

CRANE: THE POET AS HERO

An Encomium Twenty Years Later

ANYBODY who knew Hart Crane will come away from his letters both depressed and relieved. I confess that I hope I shall not have to follow again the melancholy course of this desperate life. I prefer to cherish, after the violence and final frustration of a great lyric poet, an image of Crane the poet as hero. What at last destroyed him one cannot quite say, even after the copious evidence that Mr. Weber's ably edited volume[1] puts before us. The clue to the mystery is not here: it seems to lie far back of the written testimony of the letters, in his boyhood, when at eleven he became the "bloody battleground" of his father's and mother's "sex lives and troubles," which ended not only in divorce but in such disorder that the boy was set adrift. The family was by no means poor, but he was not sent to

1. *The Letters of Hart Crane, 1916–1932*, ed. by Brom Weber (New York, 1952).

[152]

college; he was turned loose in New York when he was seventeen.

What astonishes me in the early letters—and what I had not got from Crane himself or from Mr. Philip Horton's excellent biography[2]—is not only the intellectual precocity but the precocity of moral insight. He was seventeen when he wrote to his father from New York:

When I perceive one emotion overpowering to a fact, or a statement of reason, then the only manly, worthy, sensible thing to do, is build up the logical side, and attain balance, and in art—*formal expression.*

In 1926, nine years later, he wrote to an anonymous friend:

. . . with the sailor no faith or such is properly *expected,* and how jolly and cordial and warm. . . . Let my lusts be my ruin, then, since all else is fake and mockery.

The intellectual deterioration came more slowly. What had happened to him morally between 1917 and 1926? The letters definitely answer this question. He had been confirmed in his homosexuality and cut off finally from any relationship, short of a religious conversion, in which the security necessary to mutual love was possible. I was surprised, after two years of correspondence with him, when in 1924 I met him and learned a little later that he was a homosexual: he had none of the characteristics popularly attributed to homosexuality. The violence of his obscenity (particularly about women) and his intense emotional attachments to women his own age (not to middle-aged women) convinced me even then that he was an extreme example of the *unwilling* homosexual. It is significant that his last love-affair, quite real if not wholly "committed," was with a woman; his letters to her are in every sense the

2. *Hart Crane: The Life of an American Poet* (New York, 1937).

letters of a man to a woman down to the full implications of physical love.

I dwell upon this part of the record because beneath it lies the mystery of the disintegration, at the age of thirty-two, of the most gifted poet of his generation. The "causes" of homosexuality are no doubt as various as the causes of other neuroses. But the effect on the lives of its victims seems to be uniform: they are convinced that they cannot be loved, and they become incapable of loving. This is not to say that they are incapable of strong affection: they are incapable of sustaining it in a sexual relationship. They may have affection *or* sex, but not both; or if both, both are diluted and remote. Crane's intensity excluded this compromise. Incidents of the "bloody battleground" that he told me and other friends about in the late twenties have never appeared in print, and this is not the occasion to recite them. Is it not reasonable to assume that the hatred and suffering that accompanied the violent sex-life of his parents were the decisive force that gave him eventually the homosexual neurosis? Was it possible for an eleven-year-old boy, or for the man later, to dissociate hate from the sexual relation with a woman? Possible for most men, but not, under all the conditions of his childhood, for Crane. Almost to the end of his life he was still trying to "explain" himself to his mother and to force from a peculiarly stupid and selfish woman the recognition and love of what he was. He could still love her because he could not be her lover.

It has always seemed to me that the defection of his mother precipitated the final disaster. He had been endowed with powerful family affections that were progressively frustrated. His letters to his divorced parents are among the most considerate, tender, and moving in literary history. He turned to his friends for the totally committed love, the disinterested *caritas*, that only one's family can sustain and that alone will condone repeatedly violent and aggressive conduct. None of us was capable in the end of taking the place of his family—and that was what he demanded of us; our failure—and I speak now not only for myself but, not improperly, I think, for his entire intimate circle—also contributed to the final disaster. But there was for us no other way: we also had families and our own lives.

Out of these conflicts, which in the end became one conflict, emerged a peculiar focus of the intelligence and sensibility that represents "modernism" in its extreme development. (Towards the end he speaks of himself as the "last romantic.") He had an abnormally acute response to the physical world, an exacerbation of the nerve-ends, along with an incapacity to live within the limitations of the human condition. It has become commonplace to describe this as the mentality of "alienation." But the point to be borne in mind—and it is amply confirmed by the letters—is that Crane was never *alienated*. He did not reject, he simply could not achieve, in his own life, the full human condition: he did not for a moment suppose that there was a substitute for it. This is borne out not only by his poetry—for example, *The Bridge* is not in intention a poem of "rejection," in the tradition of Rimbaud, but of "acceptance," an attempt to assimilate a central tradition; it is confirmed also by his life, reflected day by day, year after year, in the letters. His deepest friendships were not with homosexuals; they were with Malcolm Cowley, Slater Brown, Kenneth Burke, Gorham Munson, Waldo Frank, and myself; it was with these men that he lived the life of the mind and the imagination. He could not pretend that the alienated society of the committed homosexual was complete; for this unhappy person—for his epicene manners and for his irresponsibility—he felt compassion and contempt. There is a Christian commonplace which says that God does not despise conditions. Out of the desperate conditions of his life—which included almost unimaginable horrors of depravity and perversity of will—he produced in the end a shining *exemplum* of uncompromising human dignity: his poetry.

He came to New York at seventeen equipped with an hysterical and disorderly family, almost no formal education, and the cultural inheritance of a middle-western small town; his religious training had been in Christian Science. By the time he was twenty-five, before *The Bridge* had scarcely been conceived, he had written a body of lyric poetry which for originality, distinction, and power, remains the great poetic achievement of his generation. If he is not our twentieth-century poet as hero, I do not know where else to look for him.

EZRA POUND AND THE BOLLINGEN PRIZE

WHAT I SHALL say here is not in further commentary on Mr. William Barrett's article in the April 1949 issue of *Partisan Review;* nor is it the "rational, impersonal, and calm justification" of the award of the Bollingen Prize to Ezra Pound which Mr. Barrett was kind enough to expect from me. I intend rather to set down my own reasons for voting for *The Pisan Cantos*. I shall have in mind the *Partisan* symposium on the award without, I hope, being influenced by it in reconstructing my views of last November.[1]

From the time I first read Pound's verse more than thirty years ago I have considered him a mixed poet. In an essay written in 1931,[2] on the first thirty Cantos, I expressed views which the later accretions to the work have not changed: the work to which I helped to give the Bollingen Prize is formless, eccentric, and personal. The Cantos are now, as I said then, "about nothing at all." They have a voice but no subject. As one of the commentators on Mr. Barrett's article put it, they have no beginning, middle, or end. I used similar language in 1931. It is a striking fact that in talking about this work one must say "Canto XX of the *Cantos*"; there is always a Canto of Cantos, not a Canto of a substantive work with a title like Canto XX of the *Purgatorio* of the *Divina Commedia*.

Mr. Pound is incapable of sustained thought in either prose or verse. His acute verbal sensibility is thus at the mercy of random flights of "angelic insight," Icarian self-indulgences of prejudice which are not checked by a total view to which they could be subordinated. Thus his anti-semitism—which, as Mr. Auden has said, all Gentiles have felt (I have felt it, and felt humiliated by it)—his anti-semitism is not disciplined by an awareness of its sinister implications in the real world of men. Neither Mr. Pound nor any other man is to be censured for his private feelings; but every man must answer for what he does with his feelings. It has been often observed that Pound fails to

1. The first award of the Bollingen Prize was made in 1949 to Ezra Pound for *The Pisan Cantos*, published in 1948; but the prize was voted to him in November 1948 by the Fellows in American Letters of The Library of Congress, who were then the jury of award. I was a member of the jury. Since 1950 the Bollingen Prize has been given under the auspices of the Library of Yale University.
2. "Ezra Pound," reprinted in *On the Limits of Poetry* (New York, 1948).

get into his verse any sort of full concrete reality. In so far as the *Cantos* have a subject it is made up of historical materials. But if there is any poetry of our age which may be said to be totally lacking in the historical sense, the sense of how ideas move in history, it is Pound's *Cantos*. His verse is an anomaly in an age of acute historical awareness.

I do not know what reasons, motives, or prejudices prompted the other affirmative votes. There has been some public conjecture upon this subject, but I consider it a gross impropriety. I shall do well if I am able to speak honestly for myself. I have little sympathy with the view that holds that Pound's irresponsible opinions merely lie alongside the poetry, which thus remains uncontaminated. The disagreeable opinions are right in the middle of the poetry. And they have got to be seen for what they are: they are personal, wilful, and unrelated; and they are not brought together under a mature conception of life as it is now or ever was. I infer the absence of such a mature view in the man from the incoherence of the form; but it is only the latter that concerns me. Apart from specific objections to his anti-semitism and fascism, there is a formal principle which, if severely applied, would have been a good enough reason for voting against *The Pisan Cantos*. Not only the anti-semitism but all the other "insights" remain unassimilated to a coherent form. The assumption of many persons, that a vote for *The Pisan Cantos* was a vote for "formalism" and a vote against "vitality" in poetry, makes no sense at all to me.

There is nothing mysterious about coherent form. It is the presence of an order in a literary work which permits us to understand one part in relation to all the other parts. What should concern us in looking *at* the *Cantos* is the formal irresponsibility; in looking *beyond* the work, the possible effects of this irresponsibility upon society. (If Pound's *Cantos* expressed *anti*-fascist opinions, my formal objections would be the same; but I should think that the formlessness would make him a good Communist party-line poet.) But just as Pound's broadcasts over Radio Rome never influenced anybody in this country, and were chiefly an indignity perpetrated upon himself, I cannot suppose that the anti-semitism of the *Cantos* will be taken seriously by anybody but liberal intellectuals. Anti-semites will not "use" it. It is too innocent. I take it seriously in the sense of disliking it, and I cannot "honor the man" for it, as the Fellows of the Library were charged with doing; but I cannot think that it will strengthen anti-semitism.

I respect differences of opinion on this question, about which I am not well-informed. What I have already said is enough to indicate that my vote for *The Pisan Cantos* was not an easy step to take: I could have voted against it. But this is not all. I had, as many men of my generation might have had, personal reasons for not voting for Mr. Pound. In so far as he has noticed my writings at all, in conversation and correspondence—which the international literary grapevine always reports—he has noticed them with contempt.

Nevertheless I voted for him, for the following reason: the health of literature depends upon the health of society, and conversely; there must be constant vigilance for both ends of the process. The specific task of the man of letters is to attend to the health of society *not at large* but through literature—that is, he must be constantly aware of the condition of language in his age. As a result of observing Pound's use of language in the past thirty years I had become convinced that he had done more than any other man to regenerate the language, if not the imaginative forms, of English verse. I had to face the disagreeable fact that he had done this even in passages of verse in which the opinions expressed ranged from the childish to the detestable.

In literature as in life nothing reaches us pure. The task of the civilized intelligence is one of perpetual salvage. We cannot decide that our daily experience must be either aesthetic or practical—art or life; it is never, as it comes to us, either/or; it is always both/and. But as persons of a particular *ethos*, of a certain habit and character, we discharge our responsibilities to society from the point of view of the labors in which we are placed. We are placed in the profession of letters. We cannot expect the business man and the politician, the men who run the state, to know that our particular responsibility exists; we cannot ask them to understand the more difficult fact that our responsibility to them is for the language which they themselves use for the general welfare. They are scarcely aware of language at all; what one is not aware of one almost inevitably abuses. But the medium cannot be extricated from the material, the how from the what: part of our responsibility is to correct the monism of the statesman who imagines that what he says is scarcely said in language at all, that it exists apart from the medium in a "purity" of action which he thinks of as "practicality." If men of letters do not look after the medium, nobody else will. We need never fear that the practical man will fail to ignore our concern for the health of language: this he has already done by indicting Pound as if Pound, like himself, were a monist of action. Pound's language remains our particular concern. If he were a convicted traitor, I should still think that, in another direction which complicates the problem ultimately beyond our comprehension, he had performed an indispensable duty to society.

A MISCELLANY

A NOTE ON CRITICAL "AUTOTELISM"[1]

WITHOUT *The Kenyon Review* in the past ten years I doubt that we should have the New Criticism; for it was Mr. Ransom who created its myth by giving it a name. Without the myth there would not now be the decline in public favor; the decline is only a revolt against the myth. These observations ought to indicate that I do not know what the New Criticism is, that I merely acknowledge the presence of the myth. Mr. Ransom's great and actual service to us, in this period, has been his own restless exploration of the grounds of criticism and his hospitality to other writers of various points of view who have produced evidence of being seriously *engaged*. If the New Criticism differs radically from the best Old Criticism, it differs at its own peril; nothing wholly new would seem to be critically possible at a late stage of culture, such as we find ourselves in. The new thing may be the New Literature (how new it is I do not know), and a criticism sprang up to show us how to read it. Who the authors of this criticism are everybody who reads *The Kenyon Review* already knows. Its distinguishing feature hovers round the margins of the page: a hostility to, or neglect of, the "historical method." Yet in neither Empson nor Cleanth Brooks is history left out; it ceases to appear methodologically; it no longer devours the literary text; it survives as contributory knowledge. We have *The Kenyon Review* more than any other quarterly to thank for making the new "sleight" in the art of reading possible. But by concentrating the "problems" in its pages it has aroused in many of us a predictable sense of the critical limits of the

1. From a symposium, "The Critic's Business," *The Kenyon Review*, Winter 1949.

several new ways of reading the new literature, or of reading the old as if it were new.

It has seemed to me that the best criticism at all times has its best function in the ordering of original insights and in passing them on, through provisional frames of reference, to other persons secondhand. Eliot may still be our best critic because his constant frames of reference are large and loose, the frame of the particular essay being improvised, tentative and variable; he does not board the juggernaut of methodology and he keeps the faith (by and large) with the work that he is presumably examining. I am suspicious of all critical generalizations, of those that I have intemperately made in the past, and of the one that I am about to make. When insights into the meanings of a work become methodology, when the picture apologizes to the frame, we get what has been called autotelic criticism. It exists; Mr. Burke is there to prove it; but I cannot think it important as literary criticism; it has almost ceased to exist for literature (though it may *be* a kind of literature) in ceasing to be dependent.

Mr. Burke's *A Grammar of Motives* is an independent work, possibly of the imagination, and if we know how to read it, it can be both entertaining and useful; it is edifying, it enlarges one's mind. But if we think of it as criticism we must see it as an example of the atomization of experience which Blackmur feels has all but undone us. Burke seems not to be concerned with literary works as wholes; he picks off the work illustrative fractions to be devoured by his Five Master Terms. (I can think of no work of the past quite comparable to the *Grammar*, except perhaps Burton's *Anatomy*.) If there are sides to take in the little controversy which Mr. Ransom's review[2] of Hyman and

2. Stanley Hyman: *The Armed Vision* (New York, 1948), and R. P. Blackmur: "A Burden for Critics," *The Hudson Review*, Summer 1948.

Blackmur seems to invite, I take the side of Blackmur, and for a good reason: he looks like a horse of another color— roughly, of my color; that is, of almost no color at all, unless one is compelled to observe the lurid shades of the Blackmurian style. There is, at any rate, no methodology. I am the more impressed by Mr. Blackmur's almost puritanical heroism in rejecting the so-called and book sciences ending in *logy* (psychology, anthropology, sociology) because he has in the past, I believe, looked into them; whereas I never quite did. I must confess to having been a long time on his side, and not pretend that I ever had a side that he could be on. Should not criticism be one of the more prudently sceptical activities of the mind? When it reaches in Mr. Burke the stage of perverse scepticism at which it substitutes doubt of the value of the imaginative order for doubt of itself, is it not on the way to becoming a *logy?* I take Mr. Blackmur's "A Burden for Critics" to be a new declaration of critical scepticism; it may even be an augury of a rise in the market for the New Criticism. I see him here starting all over again, with accumulated knowledge and insight, but still with no commitment to "method." I agree with Mr. Ransom that Mr. Blackmur's position is untenable; it cannot be held; neither can Johnson's, Coleridge's, nor Eliot's; they are all full of holes. I hope that Blackmur will not try to hold a position and that he will continue to be interested in something else; for example, how the imagination acts in a given instance.

It would be worse than folly to argue that the whole task of criticism must stop short of its philosophical implications, or of the philosophical implications of the literary work. Any criticism that increases our knowledge of literature and its availability has its place. Only the size of the place, for those kinds that approach autotelism, is in question. The "place" of James's *Prefaces* must be larger than that of the schematization of their insights in Lubbock's *The Craft of Fiction*, even though Lubbock sharpens some of our own insights into the *Prefaces* and into James's art as a whole. There can be no end to the permutations of the critical relation to literature, philosophy, and religion. The New Criticism offers to the lingering eye as many permutations as criticism in the past has offered, and probably more. Mr. Ransom, for example, has been concerned for more than ten years with the place of the work of art in the total moral and psychic experience; and in this enquiry he has been unlike any other American critic. The New Critics look alike as Mongolians look alike to me; as Mr. Ransom might look, to the Mongolians, like the late Babe Ruth.

MODERN POETS AND CONVENTION[1]

I shall begin these remarks as if they were to be a preface to a book of my own verse. It is a kind of verse about which I know things that nobody else can know, though I daresay I shall never discover in it the things that would be good for me to know. It is, I think, a toss-up whether this kind of preface is an act of presumption or of humility. Poets insist upon writing criticism, but why they should wish to speak critically upon the occasion of their appearance as poets I do not know. Milton and Donne wrote two of the best prefatory notes in the language; they are high

1. Read at a meeting of the Modern Language Association, Richmond, Virginia, December 1936.

criticism, worth more to us today as poets than anything else before John Dryden. There is no reason to believe that Milton was uncertain of *Samson Agonistes*, or that Donne addressed Lord Craven because he doubted the value of the poems that he was inviting the reader to examine. With an envy of more confident poets that I hope is not unbecoming, I am twice diffident: I should feel uncertain in a time of poetic confidence, and I feel a special uncertainty in an age that does not allow its poets confidence in a tradition.

I do not know why other poets write; I can only suspect why I do. I know nothing of the sources and influences of my contemporaries, even when these interesting psychological and historical features of the art of poetry seem to be plain to the scholars. I ask your indulgence if, in the remarks that follow, I shall refer to my own experience. I cannot be certain even of that, and I am sorry that my comment must be negative.

No poem that I have tried to write has come out at the end according to plan. The result, which is the completed poem, ought to justify or condemn this defect of intention; but with that result I am not concerned. I am interested here in the negative fact, and I cite it because unprinted confessions of certain living poets, now to be used against them—I mean Mr. Mark Van Doren and Mr. John Crowe Ransom—point to the same hand-to-mouth poetic economy in my friends and contemporaries. That we cannot keep in view a studied end witnesses a modern impotence in the art of planned composition, a blindness to a common source of poetic understanding (if it exists), a failure to observe the proper canons of poetry. Perhaps Milton knew before he wrote a word what imagery he would use at the end of *Lycidas;* but I suppose he did not know. It makes little difference; whatever imagery he had to use, the pastoral conventions dictated the conclusion, and there was at least some restriction of choice. His departure for new pastures, after he had written the great pastoral of the language, may seem wilful, or perhaps it may cast suspicion upon his ultimate belief in its conventions as the stay to a final and self-contained form. Allow Milton all the scepticism here that you will, and he would yet have considered our total lack of conventions a mystery of the first order. He might have made up a little myth— as we are not able to do—to dramatize this poverty of ours, and to give it dignity.

I have not completed this observation; before I do I should like to glance at the related question of tradition in poetry. I seem to understand this problem a little less every day. I only know that there are certain effects in the poetry of the past that I cannot reproduce; nor do I see them successfully reproduced in other modern verse. It is a significant discrepancy that Paul Elmer More has found between the criticism and the poetry of T. S. Eliot. The criticism exhibits an insight into the poetry of the past that Mr. More, I believe, would call profound; but Mr. Eliot's own poetry seems to be quite different from the poetry that he admires. If Mr. Eliot is a traditionalist, and I think he notoriously is, why doesn't he write traditional poetry? Why, for example, doesn't he write sonnets? The conception of tradition implicit in this view is a little like that of Mr. Pound's lady from Kansas:

> She held that a sonnet was a sonnet
> And ought never to be destroyed, . . .

Again I envy my more fortunate and more gifted contemporaries. Where shall the modern poet, for whom Eliot spoke when he said that novelty is preferable to repetition, learn anything that he can use? I have been able to learn that a sonnet always has fourteen lines and is sometimes written to Laura; yet, if one who does not understand tradition is entitled to an opinion, a tradition is not so easily mastered. I shall have to mention names. Although Miss Millay's beautiful sequence, *Fatal Interview*, makes adroit use of the best conventions of the Elizabethan love sonnet, it is profoundly un-traditional. Certain conventions of the past have not merely been used; they have dictated the quality of the language, which is a language not rooted in the sensibility of our time. The style is only brilliant *pastiche*. I should cite Mr. Ransom's "Captain Carpenter" as a perfectly traditional poem. There is no other poem like it, in style, versification, and imagery, in the whole range of English poetry. Poetry in the great tradition never has more than unimportant resemblances to the poetry preceding it. The ordinary reader, or the lover of poetry—a mysterious person, for no one speaks of a lover of physics or of the differential calculus—the ordinary cultivated reader is usually the enemy of tradition; he wants to see only what he has already seen in the past.

The life of the un-traditional poet must be the life of Riley, for his popularity, if he is a skillful manipulator of mnemonic tricks, is almost automatic. For the traditional poet the task is a little more difficult. He is a practical man, and his question is always: Where can I find something that I can use? When one of the early poems of Eliot or Pound—I have a suspicion, not being able to remember clearly, that it may, incredibly enough, have been a poem by Mr. Masefield—when one of these shocking poems appeared, Sir William Watson announced that the language of Shakespeare was good enough for him. I do not know the precise significance of the fact that Eliot's "Prufrock"—

I hope that was the poem—is closer to one of the several languages of Shakespeare than Sir William Watson's own verse. I suppose that actually Sir William Watson did not think Shakespeare's language quite good enough, since he has never used it. I find it, alas, far too good for me.

Whatever it is that stands powerfully under the language of Shakespeare, that centre of obscure luminosity that one penetrates only after a second reading, I admire at a distance, if I may be sure that I am entitled to admire it at all after thirty readings; I try to understand it as an archaeologist, picking up a piece of chased bronze, marvels at the civilization of the sixth city of Troy.

I am not exaggerating this: I can only challenge you, if you think that the style of Shakespeare, or the styleless-ness of his many styles, presents not so much a mystery of the human spirit as an opportunity for research, to try to write a play or a sequence of sonnets in one of those styles. You should have no trouble doing this, if you are the kind of traditionalist that Mr. More evidently wished Mr. Eliot to be. Your play or your sequence would be the test of your ultimate understanding of a great poet. That is the miserable test of the modern traditional poet at every moment of his career. Where, in Shakespeare or in some other giant of the past, can he find something useful? Something that he can carry on? Common sense must govern one's poetry no less than one's behavior in society. If I were appearing before you this morning in doublet and hose, you would not applaud a traditionalist who understood the sixteenth century; you would laugh at a fool. The historian of manners—and manners include poetry, which also pertains to the conduct of men in society—can tell us how men behaved in another age; but they did not behave as they did because somebody told them about it. Understanding in both poetry and manners is the practice of poetry and manners, not talk about them; as it is in carpentry and plumbing. For the forms of our behavior must express the meaning of our experience, and no poet can give us a traditional experience unless he has available for his daily use some kind of traditional behavior. A poetic convention is a kind of behavior.

It is behavior because it is a peculiar focus of language upon a realm of our experience. Much of our best second-rate poetry today repeats the language of another age, and we respond to it with that part of our sensibility that has not changed. I enjoy a great deal of this kind of contemporary verse, in the vanity that permits us to like something because it reminds us of something that is better. The effort it costs us to master Keats serves us handsomely with Mr. Masters and the late Vachel Lindsay, who give us the romantic sensibility disguised, and a little debased. This poetry is not unlike grandmother's clothes in the attic; they give us the sense of her life without the difficulties famous in grandmothers. You remember Ford's beautiful lines:

> For he is like to something I remember
> A great while since, a long, long time ago.

The living person, however dear she may be, menaces the order of our sensibility; the souvenirs of her life are the comfortable assurance that all of her but our own love is dead. And we are permitted to contemplate that love with emotions that she cannot come back to challenge.

I fear that this little allegory is no more successful than some others that I have tried to write. The living person is the traditional poet, the convention plus the individual experience; the clothes in the attic are the convention alone.

I think I am not doing an injustice to the prevailing criticism of our time when I say that much of the best modern poetry is assumed to be against this convention or that; against Victorianism; against rhetoric, against rhyme and meter, against Swinburne and the eternal verities. Many persons who write verse are either for or against them, but no modern poet who is worth half an hour's attention is against any of these things; nor is he for them. He only asks, of them as of other supposedly "traditional" properties of verse, how can I use it? A poetic convention lives only as language; for language is the embodiment of our experience in words. Donne's experience was different by two generations from Wyat's, and Donne all but destroyed a convention in which Wyat was both comfortable and great. It would be frivolous to think that Donne set out to destroy any convention whatsoever. The work of a great poet—and great poets are, like Donne, often minor poets— is a body of new conventions, a permanently intelligible order of human experience. We cannot penetrate the mind of another age deeply enough to repeat its experience: it is the task of poetry then to comprehend its awareness of the past in the experience of the present.

I leave the causes and the results of the modern poet's difficulties entirely in the air. I should misrepresent my views if I left you to infer that his difficulties are without remedy or are not a kind of advantage in themselves. I can only repeat that the achievement of a new order of experience does not consist in sensations or landscapes that no one has felt or seen before. A new order of experience— the constant aim of serious poetry—exists in a new order of language. The dodo bird in the language of Mr. Masefield would be as commonplace as the turkey whose leg I expect to eat for lunch.

THE POINT OF DYING: DONNE'S
"VIRTUOUS MEN"

As virtuous men passe mildly away
And whisper to their souls, to goe,
Whilst some of their sad friends do say,
The breath goes now, and some say no:

So let us melt and make no noise,
No teare-floods nor sigh tempests move;
'Twere prophanation of our joyes
To tell the layetie our love.

I BELIEVE that none of Donne's commentators has tried to follow up the implications of the analogy: the moment of death is like the secret communion of lovers. The first thing that we see is that lovers die *out of* something *into* something else. They die in order to live. This is the particular *virtue*, the Christian entelechy or final cause of mankind, and the actualization of what it is to be human.

The logical argument of "A Valediction: Forbidding Mourning" is a Christian commonplace. Through the higher love lovers achieve a unity of being which physical love, the analogue of the divine, not only preserves but both intensifies and enlarges. The implicit symbol of this union is the Aristotelian circle of archetypal motion. Union is imagined first as a mathematical point where physical and spiritual union are the same; then as an expanding circle of which the point is the centre. The analogy is complete when the two legs of the draftman's compasses become congruent in the lovers' embrace, so that the legs form a vertical line standing on the "same" point. Thus Donne "reduces" a Platonic abstraction to actual form by contracting the circumference, "absence," to the point, "reunion," on the human scale, of the lovers.

Logically the mathematical point precedes the circle of which it is the centre; literally it also has priority, since the lover begins his journey from the point. But the poem as action, as trope, asserts the priority of the circle, for without it nothing in the poem would move: the lovers in order to be united, or reunited, have got first to be "separated," the woman at the centre, the man at the enlarging circumference, even though the separation is further and larger union. The visual image of the expanding circle is the malleable gold, which by becoming materially thinner under the hammer expands indefinitely, but not into infinity; for this joint soul of the lovers is a "formulable essence" which abhors infinity. The material gold disappears as it becomes absolutely thin, and is replaced by pure, anagogical "light"—another Christian commonplace that needs no explanation. Donne fills his circle with a physical substance that can be touched and seen; but it is the particular substance which archetypically reflects the light of heaven. Yet all this light which is contained by the circle is only an expanded point; that is to say, whether we see the lovers as occupying the contracted circle in the figure of the compasses, or the expanded point of the gold, they always occupy the same "space," and are never separated. Space is here the "letter" of a non-dimensional anagoge; and likewise the circle widening towards infinity. Thus spatial essences are the analogical rhetoric of a supra-rational intuition.

But "A Valediction: Forbidding Mourning" is a poem, not a philosophical discourse. And since a poem is a movement of a certain kind in which its logical definition is only a participant, we have got to try to see this poem, like any other, as an action more or less complete. For an action, even of the simplest outline, in life or in art, is not what we can say about it; it rather is what prompts us to speak. The Christian commonplaces that I have pointed out are not Donne's poem; they are, as letter and allegory, material factors that it is the business of the poet to bring to full actualization in rhetoric; and here, as always, the rhetoric, the full linguistic body of the poem which ultimately resists our analysis, is the action, the trope, the "turning" from one thing to another: from darkness to light, from ignorance to knowledge, from sight to insight. This tropological motion is the final cause (τοῦ ἕνεκα) of the poem, that towards which it moves, on account of which its logical definition, its formulable essence, exists. And it is the business of criticism to examine this motion, not the formulable essence as such.

Donne's two opening stanzas announce the theme of indissoluble spiritual union in an analogy to what seems at first glance its opposite: dissolution of soul from body. First we have dying men (not one man, not trope but allegory) who "whisper to their souls, to goe"; then, in the second stanza, lovers who "melt *and* [my italics] make no noise." The moment of death is a *separation* which virtuous men welcome, and the lovers are about to *separate* in quiet joy ("no teare-floods nor sigh-tempests move"). For the lovers too are "virtuous"—infused with a certain power or potency to be realized. They have no more to fear from separation from each other than dying men from death, or separation from life. If the lovers foresee no loss, they may expect a gain similar to that of the dying men.

At this point we may pass to another phase of the analogy. Here the difficult word is "melt." I cannot find in the history of the word, even as a secondary meaning, the idea of human separation. The meanings range from change of physical identity to feelings of tenderness. Tenderness is no doubt felt by the lovers at parting, and by the sad friends at the deathbed. But it is difficult to imagine these virtuous men feeling tender towards themselves, or sorry that they are dying. They might feel some "tenderness" for or yearning towards something beyond life, i.e., union with God, the realization of their virtue. Here the analogy holds for both lovers and dying men, but here also melting as tenderness becomes very remote; and we must fall back upon change of physical identity as the analogue to change of spiritual identity. The figure has got to work in the first place this side of a remote "higher" meaning, a univocal abstraction not caught in the burning bush of rhetorical analogy. Donne is one of the last Catholic allegorists; to him aiming high is meaningless unless the aim is sighted from a point below. Thus the sense in which both dying men and lovers may be said to melt is restricted to loss of physical substance, of physical identity. The verb "to goe" applies then to both lovers and dying men; both go out of the body, yet through the body, to unite with the object of love. "To goe" thus means to join, to unite with; to "melt" must be equated with "to goe"; it means going into something other than itself. Melting and going are species of dying, but the underlying universal is affirmed, implicitly, not overtly. If lovers die in this analogical sense, they lose their identity in each other, and the physical separation is the letter of the great anagoge, spiritual union. The lover dies out of himself into the beloved in order to gain spiritual union; and spiritual union having been gained, the bodies are no longer there; they are absent, separated. The lover leaves not only the body of the beloved, but his own; and the movement of action, the trope, provides for both journeys. For "mourning" is forbidden for two reasons. They must not mourn

A MISCELLANY

because "Donne" is going off to the continent; they must not mourn, since through the letter of sexual union they pass tropologically from body to spirit, where body is left behind for another kind of journey.

The structure of the poem, *at the level of trope,* turns on the pun *to die*: orgasmic ecstasy as the literal analogue to spiritual ecstasy; physical union as the analogue to spiritual. Between these extremes of inert analogy we find the moral, or tropological, movement of the poem, the central action—the passage in actualized experience from the lower to the higher. But without this egregious pun, the whole range of the pun, at that: its witty, anecdotal, even obscene implications: without it the poem would not move; for the pun is its mover, its propeller, its efficient cause.

A grammatical peculiarity of stanza two will offer indirect support for this argument. I refer to "and" between "melt *and* make no noise." I have I believe disposed of "let us be tender" as a plausible meaning of "melt." But if that were the right meaning, the conjunction should be "but," not "and." As Donne wrote the passage (we are entitled to read only what he wrote), it evidently means: Let us pass through the body, let us "die" in both senses, *and* the loss of physical self will prevent the noisy grief of "sublunary lovers" at parting and the noisy love-making of physical union. Thus if "melt" were not an extension of the pun, Donne would probably have written "but make no noise"— a prudential injunction to protect the neighbors from scandal.

Two other features of the analogy seem to me to reinforce this reading. Why are the sad friends at the deathbed incapable of detecting the exact moment of death? Affection and anxiety account for it in life. This is obviously the first and literal meaning. But here it must be considered along with the lovers' reluctance to tell their love to the

[175]

"laity." For the logic of the poem contains a third Christian commonplace: death-in-life of this world, life-in-death of the next. The sad friends are a similar laity and the laity is the world, where men do not know the difference between appearance and reality, between death and life. But men at the moment of death, lovers at the moment of spiritual union (through and beyond the body), have a sacerdotal secret, access to a sacramental rite, beyond the understanding of the "laity" who have not had these ultimate experiences. The dying of the lovers into life and the dying of death into life are reciprocally analogous. Donne is not saying that death is *like* love, or that love is *like* death; there is the identity, death-love, a third something, a reality that can be found only through analogy since it has no name. This reality, whether of "dying" lovers or of "dying" men, is the ultimate experience. The reciprocal conversion of the one into the other is the moral motion of the poem, its peripety, the "action" which eventually issues in the great top-level significance that Dante understood as the anagoge. This is nothing less, as it is surely nothing more, than the entire poem, an actual linguistic object that is at once all that our discourse can make of it and nothing that at any moment of discourse we are able to make of it.

Index

INDEX

Dante Alighieri, 32–55, 77, 90, 94, 104, 110, 111, 134, 135, 176
De Anima, 32
De Vulgari Eloquentia, 134
Dedalus, Stephen, 9
"Defense of Poetry, The," 19, 124
Democracy, 15–16, 65
Demosthenes, 149
Denham, Sir John, 113 ff., 119
Descartes, René, 4, 5, 71
Dionysius the Areopagite, 48
Divine Comedy, The, 30, 32–55, 100, 157
Donne, John, 115–17, 121, 122, 123, 128, 129, 150, 164, 170, 171–76
Dostoevsky, Feodor, 138
Doughty, Charles M., 149
Drake, Joseph Rodman, 68
Dream of Descartes, The, 37 n., 67 n.
Dryden, John, 110, 122, 123, 129, 165
Dunbar, H. Flanders, 41

Earthly Paradise, 35
Einstein, Albert, 21, 110
Eliot, Charles W., 99
Eliot, T. S., 94, 104, 110, 113 n., 122, 144, 162, 166, 168
Empson, William, ix
Epimetheus, 24
Esemplastic Power, 108
Eureka: A Prose Poem, 60, 68, 70, 72, 75–78, 80, 81, 89, 94
Evans, Augusta, 79
Existentialism, 7
"Extasie, The," 129
"Ezra Pound," 157 n.

"Facts in the Case of Monsieur Valdemar, The," 85
"Fall of the House of Usher, The," 85, 86–89
Fatal Interview, 167
Faulkner, William, 5
Figure of Beatrice, The, 38
Ford, John, 169
Frank, Waldo, 155
From Poe to Valéry, 57 n., 93 n.

Gibbon, Edward, 149
Gilson, Etienne, 50
Glanvill, Joseph, 86

Glasgow, Ellen, 82
Goethe, 108
Grammar, 100, 104
Grammar of Motives, A, 162
Granger, Frank, 134 n., 144 n.

Hall, John, 132
Halleck, FitzGreene, 68
Hart Crane: The Life of An American Poet, 153 n.
Hawthorne, Nathaniel, 81
Henn, T. R., 131, 132
Herodotus, 98
Hieroglyphics, 133
Hill of Dreams, The, 133
Hippocrates, 23
Hitlerism, 20
Homer, 34, 124, 138
Horton, Philip, 153
Humanities, The, 97–98
Huxley, Aldous, 92
Hyman, Stanley, 162

Iamblichus, 24
Idiot, The, 108
Iliad, The, 132
Illuminative Way, 36, 42, 43, 46
Imagination, 37–38 (symbolic), 40 and 70 (angelic)
Importance of Scrutiny, The, 113 n.
Inferno, 47, 90
Ingram, Susan, 82

James, Henry, 33, 138, 164
Jansenism, 5
Jefferson, Thomas, 6, 71
John of the Cross, St., 118
John the Divine, St., 10
Johnson on English Poetry Before 1660, 113 n.
Johnson, Samuel, 7, 99, 112–30, 163
Joinville, Jean de, 98
Joyce, James, 30

Kafka, Franz, 30
Kant, Immanuel, 132
Katharsis, 147
Keats, John, 144
Kenyon Review, The, 161
King Lear, 108
Krutch, Joseph Wood, 83
"Kublai Khan," 101

Lawrence, D. H., 84–86, 139
Leavis, F. R., 113, 124, 134

INDEX

INDEX